SEEING THE HIDDEN FACE OF ADDICTION

Detecting and Confronting
This Invasive Presence

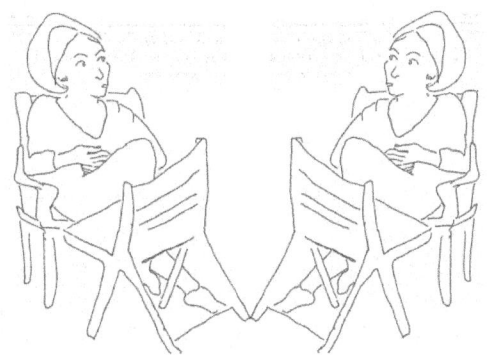

written and illustrated by
Dr. Angela Brownemiller

Metaterra® Publications

SEEING THE HIDDEN FACE OF ADDICTION

Detecting and Confronting This Invasive Presence

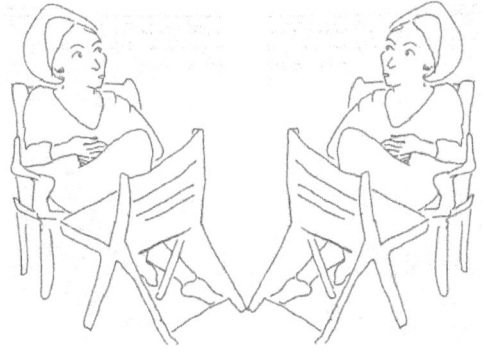

written and illustrated by
Dr. Angela Brownemiller

Publication #25
Dr. Angela® Theory and Practice Collection

Metaterra® Publications

Metaterra® Publications
SEEING THE HIDDEN FACE OF ADDICTION:
Detecting and Confronting This Invasive Presence
Copyright © 2020, 2015, 2010, 2005, 2000.
Angela Brownemiller / Angela Browne-Miller.
Copyright © 2020, 2015, 2010, 2005, 2000.
Metaterra® Publications.
All rights reserved in all formats and in
all languages and dialects known or not known at this time.
Published in the United States by Metaterra® Publications.
HYPERLINK "http://www.Metaterra.com"
www.Amazon.com
Library of Congress Cataloging-in-Publication Data.
Brownemiller, Angela.
SEEING THE HIDDEN FACE OF ADDICTION
Angela Brownemiller
1. Consciousness. 2. Psychology. 3. Biology.
4. Addiction. 5. Chemical Dependence. 6. Psychotherapy.
7. Gestalt Therapy. 8. Twelve Step. 9. Gregory Bateson.
10. Angela Brownemiller. 11. Angela Browne-Miller.

ISBN 13: 978-1-937951-12-2
(Paperback).
Also see Amazon for Ebook.
Published in the United States of America for US and worldwide distribution.
Metaterra® Publications, Metaterra.com (See this url for postal address).
SEEING THE HIDDEN FACE OF ADDICTION by and copyright © Angela Brownemiller.
Interior (book pages) and exterior (book cover):
content, text, art, illustrations, charts, diagrams, etc.
by and copyright ©Angela Brownemiller.

HYPERLINK "Info@Metaterra.com"
DrAngela.com

All rights to all copies, printings, forms, formats, editions, adaptations, and excerpts reserved. Without prior written and signed permission from the publisher, author, and illustrator, no part of this book (words, text, art, illustrations, diagrams, charts, or other) may be published, and or reproduced, copied, transcribed, distributed, transmitted, broadcast, and or stored, in any form and or by any means, (handwritten, typed, printed, spoken, taped, digital, audio, video, movie, and or other past, present, and or future forms and formats). The exception to this rights restriction is only for the inclusion of a brief (20 to 30 word) quotation (credited to this book, author, illustrator, and publisher) in a professional review. Thank you.

SEEING THE HIDDEN FACE OF ADDICTION:
Detecting and Confronting This Invasive Presence
written by Dr. Angela Brownemiller...

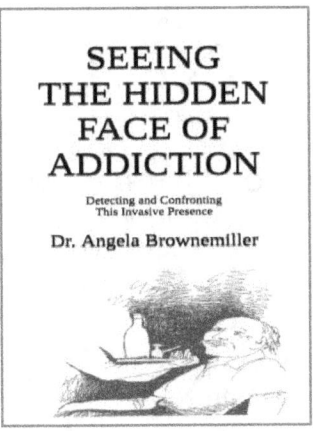

...contains material written specifically for this book, as well as modified excerpts of the following books also by author Dr. Angela Brownemiller:

GESTALTING ADDICTION: Speaking Truth to Addiction— Its Power, Definition, Theory, Therapy, and Treatment

TRANSCENDING ADDICTION AND OTHER AFFLICTIONS

See also additional research by author Dr. Brownemiller referred to in this book, SEEING THE HIDDEN FACE OF ADDICTION →

INTERNATIONAL COLLECTION ON ADDICTIONS
Angela Browne-Miller, Editor
Volume One:
FACES OF ADDICTION THEN AND NOW
Volume Two:
PSYCHOBIOLOGICAL PROFILES
Volume Three:
CHARACTERISTICS AND TREATMENT PERSPECTIVES
Volume Four:
BEHAVIORAL ADDICTIONS FROM CONCEPT TO COMPULSION

OVERRIDING THE EXTINCTION SCENARIO
Angela Brownemiller, Author

UNVEILING THE HIDDEN INSTINCT
Angela Brownemiller, Author

See also
www.DrAngela.com
for additional books by this author.

NOTE TO READERS

For all who visit these pages, note that this book talks about addiction (both drug/alcohol and nondrug behavioral and emotional addiction) in a somewhat different way. While it is not my intention to speak in science fiction-like terms, I do intend to share: a somewhat different view; a deep understanding of what is happening to the Human mind and spirit; and, a look at what role we can play in standing up to trends that may be harming us yet doing so not entirely within our awareness.

The following chapters share my sense that we are going to have to stand up to addiction as a pattern and a process not of our own making, and not entirely within our conscious control. This standing up involves seeing what is really happening to us all, detecting and then confronting what this thing we call addiction is, seeing how addiction is affecting every single one of us whether or not we feel we are experiencing addiction.

What I share herein offers a subtle yet marked shift in perspective, with easy to follow yet profound implications. To follow this slight yet major shift in thinking, both imagination and metaphor, along with science and philosophy, even spirituality, are useful tools. This combination of tools allows us to step just a little outside the box, our boxes, outside what we have somehow been led to believe about ourselves, about our addictions, and about who we actually are.

Thank you for exploring this critical yet at the same time simple perspective with me, with yourselves, with Humanity.

The stakes are higher and higher every day. It is time we stand up to forces and factors working on us so very invisibly that their powerful reality is missed.

The Author,
Dr. Angela Brownemiller

NOTE ABOUT THE FOLLOWING CHAPTERS

These chapters are designed for both Readers and Listeners, and can therefore be heard as an audio book, as well as read as a printed and an Ebook. Given these three formats in which this book is presented, some of the following material may restate itself as this book moves through its chapters.

This method not only assists with audio book "reading," this also helps many readers (whether reading print or Ebook, or hearing audio book forms) take this material in.

This approach involves allowing readers to read and or hear these ideas several times, each time being applied to a new aspect, issue, or dimension of *SEEING THE HIDDEN FACE OF ADDICTION: DETECTING AND CONFRONTING THIS INVASIVE PRESENCE.*

Table of Contents

Note to Readers	7
Note About the Following Chapters	8
1. Eyes Wide Shut to the True Nature of Addiction	13
PART ONE: NOTHING LIKE ADDICTION TO TEACH US	**17**
2. Nothing Like Addiction to Teach Us	19
3. Introduction to Seeing the Hidden Face of Addiction	21
4. Like a Virus Addiction Reaches	27
PART TWO: UNVEILING ADDICTION FOR WHAT ADDICTION IS	**31**
5. Addiction Inhabits	33
6. Seeing the Hidden Face of Addiction Programming	43
7. Seeing the Brain's Programmed-In Reality or Form Completion (Even Denial) Process	47
8. The Trojan Horse Camouflaging The Truth about Addiction	59
9. The Identified Addict	63
10. Deleting This Thing We Call Addiction	71
PART THREE: COMING FACE TO FACE WITH THE INVASIVE PROGRAM	**81**
11. Note About Chapters in Part Three	83
Process Steps Overview Charts	85
12. Recognizing and Facing the Invasive and Ingrained Problem Addiction Matrix	93
13. Patterning and Pattern Awareness Concepts	105
14. Undrugging the Feelings	113
15. The Going Conscious Process	125
16. GestaltING the Addiction	135
17. Addiction GestaltING Itself	143
18. Seeing the Presence and Power of Multiple Paradoxes	159
19. Navigating the Emotional Terrain in GestaltING	163
PART FOUR: LET'S NO LONGER BE BLOCKED FROM SEEING THIS	**173**
20. No Longer Be Programmed to Be Oblivious	175
21. Epilog: The Truth About Us	177

Booklist and Recommended Reading — 183
About the Author — 185
Metaterra Publications — 185

Illustrations, Diagrams, Charts

Trigger-Urge/Craving-Response Cycle:
    One Basic Pattern of Addiction:
        We Must Ask: What Lies Behind This Pattern? — 11
"I see you addiction, here in the chair." — 17
"Addiction, I see past your mask." — 31
Basic Form Completion Diagram — 48
"Addiction, I see you now." — 81
Four Basic Patterns — 106
Patterns Can Be Found Within Patterns — 107
Paradox Pattern Can Hold Us Stuck, Trapped — 108
Energy Held in Paradox Can Be Carefully Released — 109
A Lifetime Can Be Mapped According to Patterns — 110
Insight Patterns Can Lead to Elevation Patterns — 111
Reality Completion Diagram — 116
Infected Reality/Form Completion at Work — 118

***

Can I Separate from My Addiction? — 135

***

Chair to Chair — 147
The Client, The Addiction, and The "Empty" Chair — 149
Addiction Matrix to Addiction Matrix #1 — 150
Addiction Matrix to Addiction Matrix #2 — 151
Escape from Paradox — 158
Insight to Elevation — 164
True Problem/Challenge (Summarizing Diagram) — 171
Facings — 173
Anonymous — 181

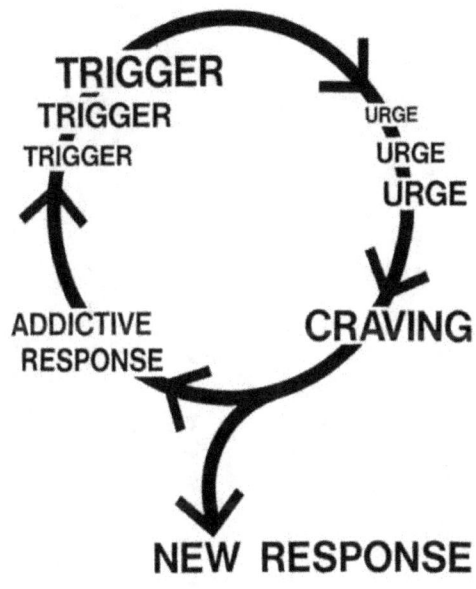

**Trigger-Urge/Craving-Response Cycle:
One Basic Pattern of Addiction**

*We must ask:
What lies behind this pattern?*

*What does it take to bring about and maintain
actual exit from such a pattern/cycle:*
A NEW RESPONSE

1
Eyes Wide Shut to the True Nature of Addiction:
What Addiction Itself Does Not Let Us Detect

Addiction is virtually everywhere. Addiction appears in a range of forms such as drug/alcohol dependence, also smoking and vaping, also gambling, gaming, shopping, spending, you name it. In our times, rarely if ever does a week go by when we do not hear news of yet another addiction-related event (a death, an accident, a finding, a treatment, a well known personality sharing an addiction-related experience, a parent or spouse or co-worker or friend or addicted person him or her self recounting a story or issue). By now, we are rather used to hearing about addiction issues, problems, treatments, theories, stories, personalities, and so on.

All this noise about addiction serves to inform us, to some extent, and this has its value. However, all this noise about addiction may have another effect. The effect I am talking about here is distraction, or perhaps distortion, or perhaps *obfuscation*[1] *of addiction itself*.

With all we think we know about addiction, we may be missing a subtle yet key point, a critical piece of information about ourselves: *the truth about our highly programmable nature*. This is not to say that all we are are robots, machines, that all we are are things, bio-bots, that simply follow programming, orders.

However, this is to say there are aspects of our behaviors, such as our addiction-related behaviors, that have *automatic response components* and *intricate response linkages* (whether or not we want these linkages)

---

[1] *Obfuscation* is defined as the action of making something unclear, unintelligible, obscure. For the purposes of this book, I add that this *obfuscation* brings itself about with the purpose or goal of rendering something (or even itself) undetectable, hidden, elusive.

working themselves into every part of our biology. We must detect and confront these linkages. We must look this biological wiring we carry straight in the eye.

We must ask:

Are we allowed to really see what is going on here? Does our addiction programming have us programmed not to fully see this?

Addiction itself may be having the effect of distracting us from addiction itself.

How convenient for an addiction pattern to work to remain in place, to have its pattern dominate even decisions regarding whether its pattern will continue to dominate.

It is as if we are not seeing the full nature of addiction while seeing what we think is the full nature of addiction.

This addiction program has its own agenda, works to sustain itself according to its own programming to do what it takes to sustain itself.

Addiction compels, *even addicts*, its host to maintain the addiction program which is to *addict its host*.

It is time we see what is going on here, how deeply programmed we are to be addicted. It is time we confront this programming, understand and realize in a new way, what is really taking place. And, it is time we see the way we have been seeing this—without knowing we are seeing this happening to us. It is time to better detect the actual nature of, and confront, **this invader,** *problem addiction pattern programming*.

Stand up and take yourself back. Stand up for yourself, and for all Humanity. As you do, be aware, the addiction programming itself, its matrix, may sense your presence, sense your growing awareness of what is actually taking place. Addiction programming may in essence work to <u>*ward you off*</u>, to invoke some lack or lessening of awareness back into you, and may strike back, seeking to make its control over you clear to you.

You can set the captives free, release yourself, and all of us, from programming running awry, holding onto us for its own benefit, from deep within us. Read on to understand what I mean here....

Dr. Angela Brownemiller
aka: Dr. Angela®

Part One
Nothing Like Addiction
To Teach Us

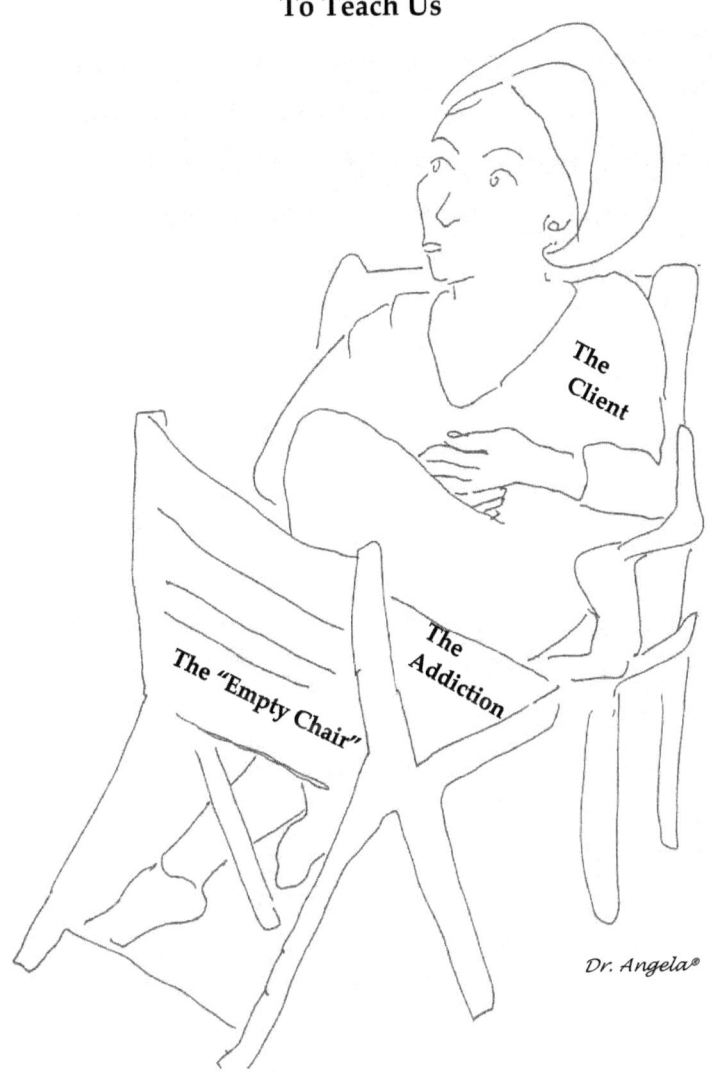

"I see you, addiction, here in the chair."

2
Nothing Like Addiction to Teach Us

How true it is that we Humans are not machines, rather are biological animals with our biological strengths and weaknesses. But wait, rewind this conclusion and listen more closely: We are not machines, yet, oddly we *are* a little like machines, or better stated, we are rather like programmable robots, biological robots, bio-bots.

There is nothing like addiction that can so pointedly reveal this to us, can so clearly reveal us to ourselves. Addiction tells us: somehow there is a glitch in our system. We Humans are wired with programming to build patterns into ourselves, life supporting and protecting patterns, yes, and also *un*healthy patterns.

Whether healthy or unhealthy patterns, they all burn themselves into us, hold us trapped within themselves. We obediently stay trapped in these patterns, run with these patterns, somewhat like hamsters in cages running on endless circular wheel tracks.

Some of the patterns we can get trapped in are quite dangerous, even life threatening (some drug/alcohol addictions, for example). We may find ourselves racing, with no apparent exit, deeper and deeper into a downward cycle, like ants parading into their death spirals. And these ants, well, these ants are wired to be *obediently* parading into their no exit traps.

We Humans are not free of such programming. We risk parallel behaviors, parallel obedience, as we move ever more deeply into various downward spirals (such as troubled, even at times life threatening, problem addiction patterns, dangerous and damaging problem behavioral and problem emotional patterns).

This wiring, this programming, that we carry so deeply within us, that we are wired to form and follow: this is the *HIDDEN FACE OF ADDICTION*.

3
Introduction to Seeing the Hidden Face of Addiction

This book is ultimately a conversation with addiction itself, seeking to pull down the disguise, to reveal addiction for what it is. You see, the truth is out there, or best to restate this, the truth is in here, deep within our minds/brains, and our SELVES.[2]

In the flow of this conversation on the following pages is addiction to substances, and to behaviors whether or not these involve drugs/substances. Included in the addictions I refer to herein are not only behavioral patterns, cycles, habits, but also emotional and even cognitive and perceptual patterns, cycles, habits.

I have come to see problem addiction as an **opportunistic matrix,** an **invasive patterning,** working its way so very deeply into our brain's networks that it can **invade and even subsume our basic**

---

[2] See recommended reading list at the end of this book. Also note, I delve more deeply into the functions of the mind/brain (and their effect upon our realizing who and what we are) in other of my books, such as: TRANSCENDING ADDICTION AND OTHER AFFLICTIONS, and GESTALTING ADDICTION — SPEAKING TRUTH TO ADDICTION, also the four volume series which I edited, the INTERNATIONAL COLLECTION ON ADDICTIONS. See also the sections on the brain in OVERRIDING THE EXTINCTION SCENARIO, PART ONE: DETECTING THE BAR ON THE EVOLUTION OF THE HUMAN SPECIES and in UNVEILING THE HIDDEN INSTINCT.

and even executive mental functions (such as thought organization, decision making, and moral judgement).

More than this, addiction can be so invasive it can even consume pieces of our own Identity, causing us to almost believe that *we are the addiction itself, that it is part of us, that it IS US.*

**At some point the boundaries
between ourselves and our addiction programming
are being compromised, confused.**

LET'S NOT
FOOL OURSELVES

We are all addicts. We all carry addiction programming. We are lifeforms that function according to deep programming, even according to *programmed-in addiction to our deep programming*.[3] Yes, environment plays a central role in all we do and are. However, we are all wired, biologically, even genetically, to develop the neural wiring that programs us to live and adapt within our environments. In essence, *we are programmed to be programmed*, to form patterns of behavior. None of us escapes this programming as this is part of how we function, and *dis*function.

---

[3] I share a more creative and philosophical discussion of this programming in UNVEILING THE HIDDEN INSTINCT. See reading list at the end of this present book, SEEING THE HIDDEN FACE OF ADDICTION. Also see the theoretical discussion I offer in several books such as: TRANSCENDING ADDICTION AND OTHER AFFLICTIONS; and the INTERNATIONAL COLLECTION ON ADDICTIONS; and also GESTALTING ADDICTION— SPEAKING TRUTH TO ADDICTION, for more information.

PROBLEM ADDICTION
vs.
HEALTHY ADDICTION

Much of this programming has definite survival and functional value. I therefore frequently use the term, ***problem*** *addiction,* to differentiate between healthy addiction programming and ***un*healthy *problem*** addiction programming (the latter, the ***un*healthy**, is programming to develop and maintain ***un*healthy *problem*** patterns).

In essence, our deepest programming to become so very addicted is running awry in far too many instances. Hence, we see too many of us falling prey to drug/alcohol, behavioral, emotional, cognitive, and other types of troubled and dangerous patternings, cycles, habits, addictions.

WE HAVE SEEN THE ADDICT:
HE/SHE/IT
IS <u>NOT</u> US

Let me emphasize this: We may *appear* to ourselves and others to be the addict, not so much because we are indeed addicted, rather because the problem addiction programming has infiltrated, even overtaken, pieces of us—invaded, subsumed, us:

> **become more and more of**
> **who we are (or feel we are).**

I have found this notion of invasion, of *infiltrating right down into the Identity,* to be highly relevant in working with persons who are experiencing problem addictions. I have seen that we are treating, speaking to, the person, yes, but also to the invading programming.

> Calling this invader out
> brings us face to face
> with the programming[4]
> holding us hostage.

NOTE: *This is in no way denying personal responsibility for doing everything possible to counteract this addiction programming. This IS however saying we must better understand what is taking place inside us when problem addiction works its way into and through us, our minds, brains, bodies, and lives.*

BEING TRAPPED IN DANGEROUS PATTERNS OF PROBLEM ADDICTION

Where we Humans have perhaps stumbled most, even at times suffered most, is in our impulse control and automatic response areas and functions. This has become ever more clear as we have struggled as a species with drug and alcohol (and other, nondrug, behavioral and emotional) addictions and patterns. We Humans can find ourselves trapped in problematic even dangerous patterns, not fully seeing what keeps us trapped there, which is:

---

[4] I have elsewhere discussed in great detail our programming to form patterns, habits, even to become addicted, and the survival value of this programming as it allows us to form healthy patterns, habits, and addictions. I also elsewhere explain how our brains are running awry, where this programming can also turn to self harming patterns and addictions. I define this programming as our **addict-ability** in other publications such as in the chapters on the brain in OVERRIDING THE EXTINCTION SCENARIO, Part One.

> our programming to be
> highly addict-*able*
> and to remain
> *trapped in*
> behavioral, emotional, and cognitive
> addiction patterns.

Here is where the concepts and therapeutic experiences I have developed and share in this book are key. These understandings and therapeutic processes can, with proper, ethical, and highly skilled therapeutic guidance, lead to ongoing corrective (and even life-changing) adaptations in perception and then in behavior.

TRUTH ABOUT US

The *Epilog* at the close of this book is titled, *The Truth About Us*. I certainly hope that ideas unveiled here in this book serve as not the last word but rather as seminal, an invitation to ever greater realizations and AHA moments, truths about us, our minds and brains, our programmings, our addictions, our **selves**.

4
Like a Virus, Addiction Reaches

We are quite aware of viral conditions and diseases that can spread around a room or across the globe. Greatly appreciated advances in modern medicine are powerful and very much needed to protect us as we face the ever changing *viral landscape*.

The term, *viral*, has taken on so many medically defined and other meanings. Of course, the basic definition of *viral* refers to that of a medically defined *viral* infection. Popularized uses of the term, *viral*, can include something that can spread or circulate widely and rapidly, which can also be a message, or an image or tune or video or some other program, rather than a virus that itself infects only a biological body. Clearly, no matter what its form, contagion or other forms of distributing or circulating the virus are key in the virus' viability and success, as the virus **relies on its host to survive** and to spread.

CONTAGION FUNCTION

Now of course, addiction (which is actually the ***addiction pattern program/matrix*** I speak of in this book) is not itself seen as *viral* from either the traditional (medical) definition or the more modern popular and or cyber/virtual technology perspectives. However, in the view of this book, SEEING THE HIDDEN FACE OF ADDICTION, we can think of the **pattern** of problem addiction, the *programming* to be addicted even to problem patterns, to begin to view the *addiction pattern itself as having a* **spread or contagion function as does a virus**.

Whether as a metaphor for *virus*, or as its own form of *virus*, the problem addiction program/pattern can be worked with, identified and confronted, in terms of its being viral, an invasive virus.

FEW ARE UNTOUCHED

All who know problem addiction patterns know how these patterns not only affect the addicted person, but also *those around that person*. It is difficult to be unaffected by the problem addiction pattern of someone near us, even if this affecting is taking place quietly, invisibly, unbeknownst to those being affected.

I say *unbeknownst* here as there are *levels of not knowing* that another person's problem addiction pattern is affecting oneself. Ranging from lack of information, to only slight awareness of minor effects, to denial, there are a range of explanations for seeming lack of effect, or lack of what appears to be any significant effect, of one person's problem pattern addiction upon another person.

INSIDIOUS TENDRILS

The insidious tendrils of the problem addiction pattern weave into the world around the addiction. Ultimately, addiction patterns weave into the lives of all who come into (any form of) contact with the addicted person.

While terms such as "co-addict" and "co-dependent" have emerged, these terms barely if at all depict the addiction program's agenda to reach far past the problem pattern addicted person, out into the world around that person.

This brings me to one of the central points in my work…

> The largely *stealth* problem addiction program matrix goes into its own form of *viral* to spread its effects in order to survive.
>
> Indeed, as I carefully explain to my clinical clients and to participants in my workshops, I also use as metaphor the *retrovirus theory of genome invasion*, where the cell's genetic material is invaded by a retrovirus to change some of that cell's genetic *directives*.
>
> I say that, similarly, the addiction program patterning invades us, our healthy patterning, to change and overtake: too many of our brain's directives; too many of our healthy patterning functions; too many of our brain functions (such as decision making, reasoning, moral judgement, etc.); even to change and overtake as much of our Identity and Identity functions as it can invade.

Part Two

Unveiling Addiction
For What Addiction Is

"Addiction, I see past your mask."

5
Addiction Inhabits

Addiction patterns **inhabit** us, they are *not* us. For us to address these invasive patterns, we must begin to *differentiate ourselves* from these patterns.

I have developed this subtle yet powerful *differentiation process* in my work with several thousand people, and view this process as central in SEEING THE HIDDEN FACE OF ADDICTION, in the DETECTING AND CONFRONTING of THIS powerfully INVASIVE PRESENCE.

The following perspective does not in any way remove responsibility from the person experiencing problem addiction. The person remains responsible for addressing, reducing the power of, even where possible overriding and or rewiring, this:
**invasive
programming.**

I have seen it, sensed this presence, and I suggest my Readers can as well. Problem addiction programming is a glitch in the system, an *invasive presence* that has worked its way into our wiring, our brains, our bodies, our lives. In this book, SEEING THE HIDDEN FACE OF ADDICTION, I offer this view of addiction that I have developed in working with (the lives and minds of) several thousand people over several decades:

**Addiction is a <u>matrix</u>,
a <u>programming</u>,
we carry <u>deep</u> within us.**

OUR PROGRAMMING TO BE HIGHLY ADDICT-*ABLE*

Addiction patterning is of course a necessary program we carry within us. We have all inherited this program to be what I describe as highly programmable, highly ***addict-able***.

When it comes to problem addiction, everyone is at risk. It is a matter of chance what each of us is exposed to, and what particular objects, drugs, behaviors, and or emotional patterns each of us is prone to become addicted to, or believe we are addicted to.

While we may not all be prone to become addicted to the same things or behaviors or emotional patterns, we are all prone to fall into *problem* addiction patterns. Once exposed to a range of addictive drugs (yes, this term "drug" includes alcohol), or addictive nondrug behaviors, or even addictive emotional patterns, we are at *risk* of becoming addicted to these, or to drugs or behaviors or emotions like these. This risk is ever present, even in the face of potential or actual harm to ourselves or others.

Indeed, we are from the start, already out the gate, even prior to exposure, at risk of becoming addicted: We are *wired* to become addicted, ideally only in healthy ways, however this is not the case for far too many persons.

The neuropathology of addiction tells us that addiction (what I am herein calling *problem* addiction) is a complex brain disorder, generally a chronic relapsing condition, bringing about lasting brain changes with mental health and cognitive adaptations and consequences. As described by the U.S. National Institute on Drug Abuse (NIDA), most addictive drugs…

"target the brain's reward system by flooding the circuit with dopamine ... a neurotransmitter present in regions of the brain that regulate movement, emotion, cognition, motivation, and *reinforcement* of rewarding behaviors. When activating at normal levels, this system *rewards* our natural behaviors. Overstimulating the system with drugs, however, produces effects which **strongly reinforce** the behavior of drug use, teaching the person to repeat it."[5]

SAME PROGRAM, RADICALLY DIFFERENT AGENDA

After so many hours, months, and years *in the room* with problem addictions, as well as with the clients these problem addictions *inhabit*, it has become clear to me that the *addiction is a presence in itself, and has a logic, a purpose, a matrix/mind of its own.* **(Yes, I use the notions of the *addiction's presence* and of the *addiction matrix being a presence* as metaphors for what is taking place, which is an *invasion of us*. Even the notion of *invasion by the addiction matrix* is a metaphor. Yet, here we have the fine line between imagination, literary device, psychological tool, and reality, as the chapters of this book explain.)**

I use the phrase *in the room* here as, when working with clients experiencing problem addictions, there are times I have clearly sensed the *presence* of the *addiction within the client – some form of powerful yet elusive presence (or phantom or ghost perhaps)*. This presence is a *self-perpetuating biochemically and bioelectrically formed*

---

[5] NIDA, *The science of drug use and addiction: the basics.* 2018. <druguse.gov> See < https://www.drugabuse.gov/publications/media-guide/science-drug-use-addiction-basics> [Italics and emphasis of terms in this quotation added by this author for purposes of this book, *SEEING THE HIDDEN FACE OF ADDICTION.*]

and reinforced neural pathway and brain process/function, or what I call a **problem addiction <u>matrix</u>**.

I have developed this *addiction matrix detection and confrontation process* I share in this book to assist us in SEEING THE HIDDEN FACE OF ADDICTION. Seeing, sensing this hidden face, this presence, is coming to know this *matrix* as an invader, an invasive program/pattern:

- This invasion is so very effective given its obscure (*under the radar*) micro level of attack. Deep within our brain's neural workings, *below the radar of our awareness*, this invasive problem patterning wields its power.

- This is indeed an invasive program, a presence, a matrix.

- This presence is so very PRESENT that I feel it sees me see it.

- And then, it feels me work with the person, with the client, to move (the idea, the concept of) this presence outside this person's/client's SELF, at least for a while.

- Then, I work with the person, the client, who senses this process and works with this concept to find, to *discover*, him or her SELF behind, *separate from*, the invader and the invader's pressure to let the problem addiction program rule.

> **We must see and speak to this addiction matrix.
> We must stand up to (and resist, *disallow*) this
> programming we carry: this programming of us
> to allow this problem pattern matrix,
> this problem addiction,
> to merge with us so deeply that
> *it feels to us to be us.***

NOT SCIENCE FICTION

I do not mean to be science fiction-like about this, however it may help to use the imagination to see/sense this concept: there is an invader present. The problem addiction is an invasive program that has worked its way deep into us, into our *selves*, our friends, our families, our communities, our colleagues, our clients. I say *invasive* as our very identities are being invaded.

Certainly we can describe this invasion in other terms; however, the *metaphor of invasion* can be powerful if carefully applied in working with people experiencing problem addictions.

This is not the healthy life-oriented programming to form healthy habits, cycles, addictions to healthy behaviors and patterns. *This is something <u>masquerading</u> as the <u>same</u> programming, yet it is <u>radically different</u> in its agenda.*

INHABITS US

When I say addiction INHABITS us, I am referring to several levels of this INHABITING. Problem addiction programming works its way into us via several standard and typically healthy pattern programming avenues, such as the following:

OUR INHERITED PROGRAMING
TO BE ADDICTED TO
BASIC NECESSARY BEHAVIORS:

This is the programming we carry deep within us, within our genes and then within our highly programmed-in yet highly environmentally-responsive brain and neural *wiring*. This is programming to be addict-*able*. As I noted earlier, being highly addict-able of course has both convenience and survival value. Whether it be eating when nutrition is scarce and finally available, or moving away from danger such as fire or a predator, we best respond relatively automatically.

OUR INHERITED PROGRAMMING TO BECOME ADDICTED TO NEW BEHAVIORS:

A second level of this programming is to take on new patterns, new habits, new cycles of behavior we are not born with. This programming clearly has some convenience and survival value, as we benefit greatly from this capability to *program in* new beneficial behaviors. This is useful, as this way we do not need to relearn every single thing we must do every single time we are confronted with a situation requiring a response from us. For example, automatically stopping at red traffic lights while driving is most definitely beneficial to us. At each red light encounter, we do not need to take the time to relearn the meaning of the light and how to stop the car. (We transfer previous learning to new situations.) So, we can just stop the automobile when we need to.

OUR INHERITED EASE OF PROGRAM-ABILITY:

However, this ease of programmability (ease of pattern acquiring) we have inherited also *leaves us open* to easily acquiring bad habits, problem patterns, dangerous addictions.

Addiction INHABITS us because the programming inhabits us: we are programmed to become *addicted to patterns*. This programming leaves us open to becoming addicted to *problem* patterns, and to *problem* pattern addictions.

WE MUST CALL PROBLEM ADDICTION OUT OF THE SHADOWS

This brings me back to the raison d'être of this book, SEEING THE HIDDEN FACE OF ADDICTION, and of other of my books where I present in depth my thinking and theories.[6] I have long seen the addict, and I see now that this addict is NOT us, but is *inhabiting us,* and not always to our benefit.

My view is that to work with ourselves and other persons who are experiencing problem drug and or nondrug behavioral and or emotional addictions, we must recognize the invasive nature of the addictions inhabiting people—inhabiting *all of us* for that matter.

We must call these addictions out from behind their masks, out from under their cover, out from their disguises as part of us, AS US.

***Addiction itself must be identified, addressed, called out of hiding, told it is to step away from the core of the person, the client, it is INHABITING.

***The person experiencing problem addiction can be helped to sense that he/she is *not* the problem addiction programming, not "the addict." Although we hear the opposite of this so many places, this mixing the individual in with his/her addiction as in, "you are an addict, admit it," this is not exactly the case. While people dealing with problem addictions can be, and best be, held

---

[6] Again note: Read in depth my theoretical and philosophical views, developments, and research in various of my books including but not limited to: TRANSCENDING ADDICTION AND OTHER AFFLICTIONS; and GESTALTING ADDICTION—SPEAKING TRUTH TO ADDICTION; and REWIRE YOUR SELF; also see the INTERNATIONAL COLLECTION ON ADDICTIONS.

accountable for their behaviors, the understanding that *their identities are not their addictions* is essential. This is what this book, SEEING THE HIDDEN FACE OF ADDICTION, is telling us.

***We can guide clients to explore the notion of ever further *differentiating themselves* from their addictions, to see themselves as not the addict, but as the person seeking to expel (or at least control) the invasive problem addiction programming.

***The addiction itself has to be related to, addressed, as an *invader* seeking to sneak in while appearing as someone's own addiction, sickness, even as part of someone's own SELF.

***The addiction is not you, nor your friends, family members, community members, nor your clients. Rather:

> **the addiction is an invasive program**
> **that is *occupying* your, our,**
> **(and your client's) mind and body.**

NOTE AGAIN:
This perspective does not in any way remove responsibility from the person, whether this is you or others or your clients, experiencing problem addiction. Each of us remains responsible for addressing, reducing the power of, rewiring, even where possible deleting, this...

> **invasive programming.**

***

The addiction is in the room. We do best to begin to call the addiction out of its hiding within ourselves, within others, within our clients. In this sense, we best help the circle of persons facing their addictions *to see and separate themselves, their identities, from the invasive addictions* that have overtaken so many parts of them.

This can allow the mind, brain, and body to begin to substantively reorganize itself and its Identity. This can allow a person to begin to, as I teach my clients, redraw and strengthen *personal boundaries*, to redefine, redraw the *circle of self*.

***

We are all at risk of invasive problem addiction programming grabbing hold of us, creeping into and then dominating our attention, our reasoning, our moral judgement, our decision making, our Identity, our Force of Will. Not one of us Humans can look away from this *deep biological glitch* we all carry: our "natural" and would be healthy addict-ability running awry.

6
Seeing the Hidden Face of Addiction Programming

This thing we call *addiction*, whether it is *problem* addiction or *necessary* healthy life-supporting addiction, is so deeply embedded, so entirely ubiquitous in its presence and reach, that it is often a given we simply accept. Indeed, we accept many of our more subtle programmings, deeply invasive addiction patterns, largely without thinking about what is taking place behind the scenes, deep within our wiring and programming.

Chances are that: we are all carrying some problem addiction patterning, most of it operating out of our conscious awareness. Chances are that: countless problem energy, neural, enzymatic, and or thought, emotional, and or other patterns are always forming and running within us and affecting our well-being in various ways.

For the most part, these problem patterns remain *hidden, implicit, out of our awareness*. Some of these patterns do emerge into our awareness when they manifest *obvious, explicit* drug/alcohol addictions and nondrug addictions (such as those to gambling, gaming, spending, shopping, and to various emotional and behavioral patterns).

BEING
ADDICT-ABLE

Being *addict-able* is an ever present always active program we are coded, wired, to carry within ourselves. Indeed, this thing we call addiction digs into us so very deeply it *disguises itself as us*. Oh yes, this thing we call addiction is the ultimate Trojan Horse quietly sneaking into us. While sneaking into us, this Trojan Horse is actually pulling us into itself, ***invading us through us***. We miss much of what is taking place as the addiction patterning itself, the **addiction program matrix**, has both life protecting and life threatening sides (*sides frequently disguising themselves as each other, and as US*).

Ultimately, we are creatures of habit, of patterning, with very little exception. We do not recognize ourselves as so very addict-able, habituate-able, program-able. Yet we are all so very much so: we are all carriers of genetic programming to form our neural wiring operating and directing our every thought, idea, emotion, and action. [Certainly our programming and wiring interacts with environment to function (to identify, intake, and process data, also acquire nourishment, respond to triggers, etc.), yet this programming to be addict-able is wired right into us, as if we are programmed bio-bots.]

HOW CAN WE SEE THIS

These days, we say we know so much about addiction problems. Yet, clearly there is more to know, to say, to do about problem addiction.

How can we see the most powerful yet most hidden face of problem addiction as it works its way so deeply into us, into our lives, and into our wiring, into our minds and brains? We have to learn to detect and then confront this presence. We have to find a way to see far more about problem addiction, far more about its hidden face/s, than our problem addiction programming allows us to see.

We must detect the *whole picture,* see that addiction is hiding in there, masking itself. And then, we must call this addiction program out from its hiding within us. To begin to see (or sense) what addiction is doing behind the scenes, deep within our minds/brains, we must look beyond what is easily seen to what is hidden there within us, the underlying addiction programming itself, *the addiction program* **matrix**.

SEEING THE PRESENCE OF THIS ADDICTION MATRIX

We can and must become increasingly aware of the concept, and of the presence, of this hidden matrix, the *presence* of this invasive programming affecting us on all levels. We can and must see what is happening here. To do so, we must see beyond the mask the addiction pattern program hides behind: our SELVES.

> **We can and must call addiction out**
> **to see it, know it, <u>not</u> be it.**

COMPLETING (NOT DENYING) THE PICTURE TO SEE WHAT THIS ADDICTION IS

It is understandable that we miss so much about our addictions, even about our problem addictions. This is part of our programmed-in information processing process: We are not seeing everything while thinking we see it all or at least enough of it.

While we may be told that it is our own denial keeping us from seeing or admitting more about our problem addiction behaviors, I say that this is not quite accurate. I say this denial is the addiction program's built in self preservation function: hiding itself via our denial of its existence, of its presence, of its full nature, of its reality.

Sure, denial is a part of the story, however even denial is misunderstood. As with everything we do and think and feel, our brain, our programming, is involved in any denial process at work within us. And, while each person dealing with problem addiction is responsible for doing what it takes to address his or her addiction-related behavior, understanding what is behind the denial is important.

In working with so many clients experiencing problem addictions (to drugs/alcohol, vaping, smoking, also gambling, gaming, shopping, spending, sex, love, relationships, even moods, and more), I have found that the presence I speak of, the invasive addition program matrix, affects the brain/mind in ways that *protect, support, **enable** the addiction pattern*. In this sense, I say that:

It is the addiction program matrix that is designed to protect, support, enable itself, and thus to <u>generate denial and other means of not allowing us to see what is really happening</u> when a problem addiction pattern takes hold of us.

It is the addiction program matrix that takes advantage of our brain's function to see seemingly whole or complete pictures of its reality without really seeing what is really going on.

7
Seeing the Brain's Programmed-In Reality/Form Completion (Even Denial) Process

It is not surprising that we do not know everything there is to know about ourselves and our patterns, cycles, habits, addictions. It is not surprising that we tend to miss the early stages, subtle stages, of the shift out of our healthy patterning into problem patterning and *problem addiction to problem patterning*. We simply do not and cannot (are not wired to) see all that is going on around and within us. We naturally miss much of the detail, most of the brain's processing, all of the intricate micro level neural processing of pattern and addiction building.

Of course, it is not unusual to look at something and not see every detail. Our brain's processing functions do not have the capacity to see it all. We naturally see only some of what we are looking at. Our brain's processing functions fill in the gaps to give us the sense that we see the whole picture or enough of it.

This is a necessary (evolved or designed[7]) characteristic, one that likely emerged in the wild where detecting the presence of a predator frequently involved rapidly "seeing" or perceiving a whole picture even when there was not enough time or data to "see" the whole picture.

---

[7] I leave it to Readers to apply their own views of evolution, divine processes, intelligent design, and other theories of our origin and development. In this and other of my books, I say that: No matter how we have arrived at the condition we find ourselves in, we must become highly aware of how programmed, even programmed to develop problem patterns and addictions, we are now.

BRAIN IS PROCESSING TO FILL IN GAPS

We are basically always filling in the gaps in what we see, completing the partial picture this way:

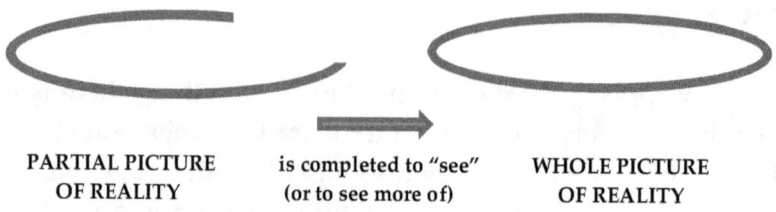

PARTIAL PICTURE   is completed to "see"   WHOLE PICTURE
OF REALITY   (or to see more of)   OF REALITY

BASIC FORM COMPLETION DIAGRAM

Understanding something about the concept of *completing a picture*, seeing the whole or more of the whole picture, is central in my work with persons experiencing problem drug/alcohol, behavioral, and or emotional patterns. This understanding is key in the DETECTING AND CONFRONTING of THIS INVASIVE PRESENCE I work with my clients to do.

THIS REALITY/FORM
COMPLETION APPROACH

In this *reality or form (reality/form) completion approach* I have developed and conduct with my clients, I say that:

We are most equipped to stand up to the addiction program matrix when we understand that this program/matrix is not only invasive but also highly elusive: designed to be hiding the truth about itself, hiding its very presence within us, disguising itself as part of us—as US.

This addiction program matrix
takes full advantage of
our brain's *Reality/Form Completion* function
to depict to us
a reality that folds the
addiction *into* us, into our beings, into our SELVES,
so as to hide its true nature,
disguise itself as US, as part of US.

This is the invasive problem addiction matrix
infecting us.

This is the
<u>INFECTION</u> OF OUR
BRAIN'S NATURAL
REALITY/FORM COMPLETION FUNCTION.

This <u>infection</u> process forms a false picture of our reality,
of our addiction patterning,
of our SELVES,
of what is happening within us,
to allow the problem matrix to
disguise its true nature,
to mask, hide, its true presence.

This concept is central in this *Reality/Form Completion Approach* I have developed in working with clients experiencing problem patterns (whether these be patterns of drug/alcohol addiction, nondrug addiction, or other problem behavioral, emotional, cognitive, and or thought patterns).

Note: In my work, I extend the notion of completing the picture of what our eye sees (such as closing the line on the broken circle) to other sensory, emotional, cognitive, and perceptual experiences. In so doing, we begin to SEE and sense more about THE HIDDEN FACE OF ADDICTION.

SEE THE HIDDEN FACE

We can begin to see the *hidden face of what we are looking at and not seeing (not seeing at all, and or not seeing all of, and or not seeing the truth about)*, **the hidden face of what we believe is ourselves.**

We begin to see, to ALERT OURSELVES TO, our brain's programming to generate a picture of reality for us—whether or not this is an accurate picture of reality—whether or not this is an accurate *Reality/Form Completion.*

We can begin to see and sense what it is that the problem addiction program matrix has formed *within* our brain, *within* our mind, *within* our Identity, while posing *as* our Identity.

BEYOND
TRADITIONAL
FORM COMPLETION THEORY

For the purposes of this book, I emphasize the importance of seeing, sensing, more and more of the whole picture as not only therapeutic but critical in work to *detect and confront* problem addiction *patterning and its programming.*[8]

---

[8] All work directed to revealing more about oneself and one's addiction programming must be done with great awareness. Too frequently, persons working with clients experiencing problem (drug, alcohol, and other)

It is this process than can detect more of what is running awry deep within our minds/brains: addiction programming becoming *problem* addiction programming. Looking at the deepest workings of our addiction functions is a challenge, as these deepest workings, internal micro level wirings, programmings, *are designed to stay under our radar.*

PROCESSES OF *REALITY/FORM COMPLETION* ARE ONGOING IN LIFE, EVEN IN PROBLEM ADDICTION PATTERNS

Seeing more about what is going on, more about what is happening to us, more of the whole picture, is *completing the picture: form completion.* Of course, in my **Reality/Form Completion Approach** as described in this book, I am building on traditional "gestalt" theories [9] of perception which refer primarily to vision and visual processing. As I note above: In my work, I extend this *visual image form* completion more broadly to a wider range of cognition and perception, beyond visual perception itself.

---

addictions say to these clients that it is *their own* "denial" that stops them from admitting more about their addictions. In this book, SEEING THE HIDDEN FACE OF ADDICTION, I suggest that it is the addiction programming that resists us knowing more about ourselves, resists us knowing that we are being inhabited, invaded, by this opportunistic matrix, this invasive addiction program patterning. We must develop greater clarity about this. *Again note: this in no way removes responsibility from the individual for doing the work of addressing problem addiction. This simply evolves our understanding of what is taking place, of what must be confronted.*

[9] I have discussed highlights of the original "gestalt" theories of perception, and applied my interpretation and extension of these original theories, in the book where I share in depth my own views and theories regarding, and further development of, the concept of gestalt. See GESTALTING ADDICTION—SPEAKING TRUTH TO ADDICTION.

We are never able to see the entirety of our realities, never able to see the whole picture. All we have is partial perceptions of whole pictures.

In order to live, we are always completing our incomplete, fragmented, partial perception of our situations, our realities, even of ourselves and our experiences of being ourselves.

WE ARE ALWAYS REALITY/FORM COMPLETING.

THE PROBLEM ADDICTION PROGRAM / MATRIX
<u>INFECTS</u> THE PROCESS OF
REALITY/FORM COMPLETION
TO SUPPORT AND PRESERVE
PROBLEM PATTERNS

This book offers this extension of original (visual) form completion theory (and its related law of closure[10]) to help us think about seeing and detecting: what we are <u>programmed</u> to (*think we*) see and <u>*what we are programmed not to see*</u>; as well as, what we are programmed to <u>*sense and not sense, know and not know*</u>. I call this a *Reality/Form Completion Awareness*. This *Reality/Form Completion* understanding can aid us in sensing and SEEING THE HIDDEN FACE OF ADDICTION, and in DETECTING AND CONFRONTING THIS INVASIVE PRESENCE.

In so doing, we can empower ourselves to make a **subtle yet profound shift in understanding what is happening to us**. We can

---

[10] For a review of components of traditional and mainstream gestalt theory of visual perception (such as the law of closure), see *GESTALTING ADDICTION— SPEAKING TRUTH TO ADDICTION.*

recognize that this *Reality/Form Completion* is always taking place, even in the realm of *our addiction-related perceptions, even our problem addiction-related perceptions.*

We can begin to *rethink what is taking place* in terms of the <u>*design*</u> *of the invasive problem addiction pattern programming* to be *deceptive*: to *pose as part of US* rather than as an *invader infecting us* — an invader with its *programming <u>of us</u>* to develop and be trapped in problem behavioral and emotional addiction patterns.

Central in this *Reality/Form Completion Approach* and this *Reality/Form Completion Process Awareness* I share in this book is the subtle yet monumental shift in understanding that is key in recognizing what is actually taking place:

1) **Frequently, it is the problem addiction pattern program/matrix** *itself* **that maintains** *control* **over the** *Reality/Form Completion Process* **that** *does not allow us to see (sense, detect) itself.*

2) **The problem addiction pattern matrix invades, takes control of,** *infects***, our usual** *Reality/Form Completion Process* **to present a distorted picture of what is happening to us, to even disguise itself as us rather than an opportunistic invader.**

3) We must recognize, detect, the possibility of, conceive of the reality of, this <u>*Infected*</u> *Reality/Form Completion*, so that we can begin to address it, confront it.

AGAIN NOTE THIS IS COMPLETING A BROKEN PERCEPTION, A BROKEN CIRCLE

Note again (and again and again) that, of course, not all *Reality/Form Completion* is masking problem addiction programming. Our brain engages in *Reality/Form Completion* much of the time. We simply do not have the brain space or band width to see everything everywhere at all times.

(Also note again: Where this form completing is the traditionally-defined visual perception process, this form completion (according to gestalt theory referred to in the footnotes for this chapter) is a **gestalt process of *form perception***[11] which basically only addresses how the eye (and visual function of the brain) perceives what it visually "sees.")

In the chapters of this book, I explain that form completion, or what I call <u>Reality/Form Completion,</u> extends well beyond the visual, that visual is a model and even metaphor for the full range of what I say is taking place, of what I describe as REALITY/FORM COMPLETION. We just do not see *or sense* all of any or everything we are looking at *or sensing*. Therefore we (our minds/brains) fill in the gaps to give ourselves a *sense* of the whole picture.

---

[11] Originating in 1920: the German word, *gestalt*, pronounced *guh-shtalt*, refers to: form, shape; an organized field, pattern, or configuration that cannot be derived from the sum of its parts; a unified whole. Plural: *gestalts, gestalten*. Derived from the German philosophy of *gestaltqualitat*, meaning form or shape, exploring the notion of perception.

> This *Reality/Form Completion Approach* that I have developed to share with my clients allows us to think in terms of metaphor. Now, when the broken circle we see (we sense) changes to the unbroken or whole circle, when we are (OR OUR <u>PROGRAMMING</u> IS) filling in the gap/s, completing the circle, we are (OR OUR <u>PROGRAMMING</u> IS) doing so on many levels.
>
> Now, what we are *experiencing* (seeing, hearing, tasting, feeling, sensing, perceiving) and are **reacting to** is not only a visual image, if visual at all, rather this is a complex multi-layered process that is generating, *even fabricating*, a perception of our reality: a set of sensations, emotions, thoughts, we *believe* (actually, OUR <u>PROGRAMMING</u> HAS US BELIEVE) we are having/experiencing.

In living, we are continuously completing a partial or broken perception, a partial or broken circle. Again, this is a natural and necessary function.

However, this process is being invaded and controlled by problem programming: this programming is completing the partial or broken circle/picture/perception in a way that serves its purposes, **sustains it, not us.**

GESTALTING

Now, let me share the term for the therapeutic (and metacognitive) process I have developed and engage in with clients coming in to *SEE* and *CONFRONT* problem addiction:

This term is *GestaltING*. I have defined this process of mental, emotional, cognitive, yes, of course psychological, biological, *reality/form completing* as a *GestaltING*. Building on the traditional gestalt theory of visual perception, on the concept of *visual* gestalt form completion as pictured earlier (via the circles diagram) in this chapter, I have, in my work over the decades, coined this verb, *GestaltING*.

I define this *GestaltING* as the *act or process* of perceiving or deriving (or detecting or revealing) a whole or more whole picture of oneself or of one's emotions, impressions, experience/s.

> This more whole picture generates the sense of having a greater understanding by allowing (or perceiving) parts to suggest (or appear to reveal) the whole (whole ***truth***) they are components of.
>
> Whether this whole that is perceived has any relation to truth is of course subjective, and even prone to INFECTION by the problem addiction program/matrix.

This *GestaltING* can work for us when we understand what is involved in *GestaltING* our perceptions, even what appear to be our addictions. This verb I have developed, *GestaltING*, thus also suggests an unveiling or **AHA process**—a *Reality/Form Completion*, closure, realization, Insight, discovery, an unveiling.[12]

In my work with people experiencing problem addictions and other parallel behavioral and emotional patterning conditions, I

---

[12] I explain this unveiling process further in other of my books such as *Volume 3* in the KEYS TO CONSCIOUSNESS AND SURVIVAL SERIES, titled, *UNVEILING THE HIDDEN INSTINCT*.

use the term *GestaltING* to label specific therapeutic processes such as those I describe in the later chapters of this book, which are the **GestaltING the Addiction Matrix Processes** I have developed in working with many people over many years.

I seek to reach beyond my and others' previous discussions and definitions of both these terms, "addiction" and "gestalt." I also move beyond old definitions of "gestalt therapy" (which itself is not gestalt theory of perception).

Let's rethink, reformat, our notions of these terms, *addiction* and *gestalt* and *gestalt therapy*. Let's step away from holding to narrow and at times confining, even distorting, definitions and applications of these terms.[13]

In the latter regard, although I do refer to what some call gestalt *therapy* in this book,[14] I seek more to reveal the nature of *any REALITY/FORM COMPLETING gestalt of anything*, and in the particular case of this book, what I describe as:

the
gestalt of
addiction itself.

---

[13] I discuss original gestalt theory of visual perception in the book where I further differentiate my work from traditional science of perception in the book: GESTALTING ADDICTION — SPEAKING TRUTH TO ADDICTION. In that same book, I also differentiate my therapeutic processes and work from the existing range of what calls itself gestalt "therapy."

[14] I come to this discussion from a different perspective, with a different goal, looking beyond simply exemplifying or teaching the practice of traditional gestalt therapy, a curriculum I leave to other settings.

CALLING THIS ADDICTION OUT OF HIDING

Again, what I am saying here is that there is more to this *GestaltING* of *Addiction* I am describing, more than directing the performing of so-called "gestalt" and "therapy" on/with patients, clients, others. I therefore seek to:

- *Gestalt Addiction Itself*,
- **call addiction out of its hiding within us, within our deepest realms, within our deepest coding to be addicted.**

This *GestaltING* **OF** *Addiction* I am doing here is calling out...
   ...addiction as an opportunistic program within us.
Again...
   addiction hides behind us, disguises itself AS us.

We can rethink our theories of, treatments of, addiction to adjust our understanding of what is happening within and to us. We can take ourselves back from a hidden invasive matrix we call addiction. We are ready to see that:

GESTALT*ING* **IS** *REALITY/FORM COMPLETING*
and that
GESTALT*ING*
THE PROBLEM ADDICTION PROGRAM MATRIX
IS *REALITY/FORM COMPLETING*
TO UNVEIL/REVEAL
THE TRUTH,
TO DETECT THE INVASIVE PROGRAMMING
INHABITING US, INFECTING US.

8
The Trojan Horse Camouflaging The Truth about Addiction

Too frequently when there is a problem addiction, this problem programming/patterning merges with us to such an extent that its treatment (in therapy, in doctors' offices, in treatment centers, in hospitals, etc.) feels to some addicted persons like an assault upon themselves—an assault taking place while they STRUGGLE to unravel themselves from this Trojan Horse we call addiction. We feel the STRUGGLE, it is real, as if the addiction itself is alive and is fighting back, seeking to stop our realizing its invasive programming is present, seeking to stop our realizing this addiction programming is NOT US.

>If we look, we can see this
>monumental tug of war
>taking place within us
>(yes, all of us).
>
>Push pull, tug toward, tug away.
>
>Here is where it becomes clear that
>we are not "our"
>drug/alcohol,
>and behavioral and emotional, addictions.
>We are not this programming,
>not this matrix,
>not this invader.

HERE IS THE DOUBLE BINDING NATURE OF ADDICTION

Revealing the invasion of us by this Trojan Horse is detecting this problem addiction program/matrix. We can see and even highlight this Trojan Horse to see/sense its *sneaking into our Identity* by invading our brain's programming. We can and must see this. Let's begin by recognizing the following:

1. This problem addiction pattern is in essence a Trojan Horse (a retrovirus-like Trojan Horse, a stealth invader) that has made its way into us by being VIEWED BY US AS US.

2. We are *not* this Trojan Horse, this invader of us, hiding within us by posing as us or part of us. We are *not* the problem addiction, we are *not* this problem addiction programming.

3. Here is the double bind that problem addiction patterns pull us into and work to hold us trapped in: **REJECTING THE PROBLEM ADDICTION CAN FEEL VERY CLOSE TO REJECTING OURSELVES.** (What a *Paradox*, a double bind, this is![15])

4. This is the *Paradox inherent* in problem addiction: we overlap with the addiction program to such a great degree that distinguishing between it and ourselves, and then separating from it, is intensely challenging and difficult.

---

[15] *Double bind* is defined as a situation in which a person is presented with two irreconcilable demands or pressures, or a choice between two undesirable options. I add that this indicates the stage I define as *Paradox*: → ←

5. So very many persons seeking to weaken or break (or let die) their problem addictions speak these words, "I feel like I am dying." Yet, when working to break a problem addiction, what may be dying is the problem addiction pattern and not the person it has inhabited.

6. The double binding problem addiction pattern seeks to hold us in its pattern program by invading even our self definition.

AGAIN THE DOUBLE BIND: WHEN WE SEEK TO END THIS ADDICTION, OUR MINDS AND BODIES CAN REACT AS IF WE ARE SEEKING TO END OURSELVES.

7. **OUR ADDICTION PROGRAM PATTERNING USES US AS ITS**

HUMAN SHIELD.

8. We must retrieve, take back, who we are from problem addiction patterns. These problem patterns can invade so many levels of us, of who we believe we are, including our Identity itself.

9
The Identified Addict

The problem addiction pattern program is a *highly elusive* invasive program: This programming of us is so elusive that the SELF can be drawn into *confusing itself with, mistaking its Identity for,* the addiction pattern programming.

IDENTIFYING
THE ADDICT AS THE "I.P."

Too frequently, the apparently "addicted person" is viewed as the "identified patient" or I.P. Of course, we know from close examination of friendships, love relationships, marriages, families, communities, where addiction issues are involved that the identified patient may not be the actual patient or at least may not be the only patient.

When addiction is in the room, it is easier to point the finger at someone else and say that he or she is the addict, that he or she is thus the identified patient needing treatment, rather than step forward and identify as the or one of the "patients."

"I.P." IS NOT THE "I.A."

Yet, we must not let ourselves confuse this I.P. label with what I term the "identified addict" or I.A., however confused these concepts may be in our thinking. Let's not allow the addiction programming to rule our own perceptions (of our own realities) and our own *Reality/Form Completions* of our realities. Let's not allow the addiction program/matrix to tell us what and who the addiction actually is. It is the problem addiction *program* that should be the called the identified addict, the I.A., not the individual *person*, not the *self* itself.

Certainly, we still want to provide treatment to persons **infected by** the problem addiction pattern programming. Yet, we must draw a distinction between the Identity of the I.P., [16] the individual patient (or as I term this, the client), and the Identity of the invasive problem addiction program which I view as being the actual I.A.

This distinction is not only fair, it is essential. Problem addiction is a chronic and frequently life damaging and life threatening brain disease, an infection by an *insidious opportunistic program*. I again say here, let us always keep in mind that...

**the afflicted individual
is <u>not</u> the disease.**

The more the problem addiction program has invaded the self, the more the self has absorbed the problem addiction pattern/program into its Identity. This makes the problem addiction very difficult, at times life and death difficult, to detect, confront, and reduce, control, leave, break free of.

---

[16] Also note, the very important discussion regarding the incorrect or biased labeling of an individual in a family as the only I.P. (when other family members may be deflecting their own possible identification/s and role/s as persons with I.P.-like symptoms) is reserved for other publications. See chapters in the *INTERNATIONAL COLLECTION ON ADDICTIONS,* and also in *TRANSCENDING ADDICTION AND OTHER AFFLICTIONS.*

> The severely addicted individual
> may have come to feel that she/he is
> "basically just a lifelong addict,"
> has a life so deeply invaded by,
> so profoundly interfered with,
> even dominated by,
> the problem addiction program/matrix
> with its tendrils
> reaching so deeply even
> into the Identity itself.

Yet, again note, **the addict *is* the addiction programming, *not* the individual this programming has invaded.**

> The addiction **is** the invasive **program**
> and **not** the program's host,
> **not** us.

THE TRUTH ABOUT
THE IDENTITY OF THE ADDICT

The identified addict is frequently viewed as the person experiencing the problem addiction to drugs/alcohol or to a non-drug behavior.

> **Yet, look again, and again note:
> the identified addict is the problem addiction
> pattern/program itself.**

PARALLEL
BOUNDARY CONFUSION

This is the *inherent confusion* that *the problem addiction pattern program is designed to generate*: the program's ***distortion of the boundaries between the self and the addiction***. It follows that the addicted person is likely to experience *boundary confusion on all levels.*

The problem addiction program seeks to *compromise the boundaries between the self and the addiction.* Other personal boundaries also *experience pressure and then parallel confusion.*

PEOPLE AROUND ARE DRAWN IN[17]

With the compromising of boundaries *within* the "addicted person," the compromising of boundaries *around* that person can also take place. It is not surprising that persons close in to an "addicted individual" are at risk of being sucked into the "addicted person's" patterns, even sucked into that person's reality. (Recall the old co-addiction adage, "*She* went to jump off the Golden Gate Bridge, and *his* entire life flashed before *her* eyes.")

When persons around the identified patient or what some will say is the identified addict are engaged in (or affected by) the problem patterns of that so-called "addicted person," all of their boundaries are weakening and blurring. This is a biochemical, an emotional, and an energetic process.

The problem pattern matrix has not only invaded the one addicted individual, the so called "addict," but frequently also has invaded the persons around that individual, the so called "co-addicts" and so-called "co-dependents." (Note: This does not say that co-addiction and co-dependence are not serious conditions to be addressed. This does however say that we must rethink our

---

[17] Refer to *Chapter 4* of this book, where addiction is described as being LIKE A VIRUS.

understanding of what drives this co-addiction and co-dependence.)

> Boundary confusion
> and boundary intrusion
> are key characteristics of this
> problem addiction situation.
>
> Addiction programming seeks to
> enroll as many as possible
> in support of this programming.
>
> Boundaries
> are thus under a great deal of pressure.
>
> The problem addiction matrix
> invades any boundaries it can.

The problem addiction pattern program is designed to (has designed itself to?[18]) reach past interpersonal boundaries into others close to the "identified patient" to lure them into supporting or even joining the problem pattern in some way that serves, supports, fuels, enables, conveniently ignores, helps maintain and *sustain* the pattern in some way.

The profound danger faced by those around a so-called "addicted person" is generally overlooked, not seen or emphasized enough.

BOUNDARY TRANSGRESSION DANGERS

Not only do co-habiting persons miss seeing some if not all of the *boundary transgression dangers* they themselves face, others outside may also not see the whole picture. I have seen this so

---

[18] I delve more deeply into the matter of matrix, pattern, even addiction, program design and evolution in several other of my books. See reading list at the end of this present book, *SEEING THE HIDDEN FACE OF ADDICTION*.

clearly in my work with individuals (and with families of individuals) experiencing problem addiction patterns: *the invasive problem addiction matrix hides its actual nature from all it touches. The profound danger faced by those around a so-called "addicted person" is highly complex. This dangerous and truly deceptive complexity is overlooked, not anywhere nearly enough understood, seen, or emphasized.*[19]

---

[19] The matter of boundaries is central, even at times life saving, for family members, especially when there are severe addictions present. I refer here to an event a client spoke of during a therapy session as she discussed her husband's severe poly-drug addictions. One morning, she was expected to join her husband on a drive out to an event. She had been avoiding being a passenger when he was driving, as he had been "drugging himself so much lately." This particular morning, she again felt she simply could not join him. When he pressured her, she told him she would only go if she could drive his car. He said no, and grew very angry with her that she was refusing to join him, and even angrier when she begged him not to go, even without her, telling him she felt he was in danger as he'd been "using" so much lately. She even went so far as to throw the car keys out into a field near their house. Her husband simply got his spare key and prepared to leave. He again demanded she join him. She hesitated a moment, almost saying yes. But she again said no and that he should not go either. When she went to take that spare key away as well, he struck her hard and threw her to the ground. Stunned, bruised, cut, and bleeding, when she was finally able to stand up, he was in the car and racing down the driveway. ... Several hours later she received a call telling her he had just been in a serious accident and was being taken to the hospital. As she rushed to the hospital she realized that: had she not objected to joining him, had she not held firm in support of her own boundary, she could have been in that accident with him. In that moment, she realized that she had to form very clear physical, emotional, even energetic boundaries around herself, to pull herself out of his problem addiction pattern for once and for all. What later became more clear to her was this: In her *GestaltING Addiction* work with me, she realized the presence of the insidious invasive addiction pattern that she had been speaking to while begging her husband not to go on that drive. "Now I see that I was married to my husband, but also to that problem addiction pattern that had invaded him. Not only would my husband not let go of me, his addiction also would not let me go."

WE JUST DO NOT SEE THE ADDICTION PROGRAM AT WORK

The addiction programming seeks to have its disguise continue. The addiction program seeks to have the addicted person and others around him/her identify the addicted person as the identified addict (I.A.) so as not to recognize the invading addiction program's expanding presence.

Again, the Trojan Horse of the problem addiction pattern matrix is so invasive, and so stealth in its invasiveness, that we do not fully see what is being invaded (ourselves), nor that an invasion has taken, is taking, place.

It is time to see this, to call, to *Reality/Form Complete*, to be *GestaltING*, problem addiction programming out of the shadows. It is time to see, to reveal, to detect, more of the whole picture. Here is where we can take a real gestalt, the *GestaltING of Addiction*, to the invading addiction program, to the Trojan Horse itself.

10
Deleting This Thing We Call Addiction

It is such a long way home, back to me.
Will anyone ever live there again?

(Anonymous Group Therapy Participant)

Problem addiction pattern programming is not going away. It may dress itself up differently, disguise its presence ever more efficiently, or seek to change (reprogram) our minds about its nature (if and when we do detect its actual nature and truly opportunistic invasive presence).

Problem addiction programming may not ever be entirely deleted. It may however be detected, and then confronted and reset, refocused, rewired, overridden.

Hello addiction program, we know you. At least we think we know you. We have been living with you and or around you for so very long now. Indeed, it is in *our* nature to form *your* addiction patterns, even in our genetic coding, neural wiring, to do so.

ADDICTION IS PART OF US

So the addiction programming is part of us, within and all around us. And yes, so far as we know, "it" (this "problem") is not going to go entirely away. But, what is this "it" that is not going away? What is this "it" we are looking at here? Can we see this "it"? Can we define this "it"? Can we know this "it"? Can we talk to this "it" as "it" lurks within us?

I say yes: we can detect, call out, see, go ahead and *form complete*, and then take through a *GestaltING Process*, this "it," this addiction program matrix (as exemplified in later chapters of this book). We can even have this "it," this addiction program, *gestalt itself* (also as exemplified in later chapters of this book).

Can we come face to face with this IT? Can we call this IT out of the recesses of ourselves? I say YES.

PROBLEM ADDICTION PROGRAMMING: DO YOU EXIST?

ARE YOU OUT THERE?
ARE YOU IN HERE?
CAN I TALK TO YOU?
CAN I SEE YOU?
YES.

AM I YOU?
ARE YOU ME?
NO.

Your problem addiction program, its problem addiction pattern, is **not** you; however, **unraveling your addiction programming from yourself** is a challenge for so many reasons. Although we are not our biological bodies, we identify with our biological bodies so very much that untying a problem addiction program from within our bodies and brains can feel like cutting out a piece of ourselves.

SURVIVAL REQUIRES SOME PROGRAMMING

We are biological life forms, animals, programmed for what were once likely only survival oriented reasons to become addicted to yes, necessary, yes, survival oriented behaviors.

We have maintained this innate capability to addict to necessary behaviors for generations, for long phases of our evolution or development, most likely, if I might suggest this, even since our (design and) genesis. (I leave it to Readers of this book to interpret *genesis* and *design* according to their own preferences and beliefs.)

If we look at this remarkable programming phenomenon, at this great convenience, we perhaps should be grateful that our species has survived thus far here on this planet Earth. And we should perhaps thank our lucky stars that we are programmed to become addicted to necessary, even survival oriented, behaviors. Again...

**WE ARE ALL
HIGHLY PROGRAMMABLE LIFE FORMS,
BEINGS GENETICALLY CODED
TO BE RECEPTIVE TO
PROGRAMMING
THAT ALLOWS US
TO BECOME "ADDICTED" TO BEHAVIORS
WE NEED TO HAVE
FUNCTION AUTOMATICALLY
IN ORDER
TO ALLOW US
TO SURVIVE.**

This program-*ability* is a great success for our species, as for many others: we are still here, walking this planet. We even know (consciously in some ways, and then sub- and unconsciously for the most part) how to program ourselves to function in this modern world, to ride a bicycle, to stop automatically at those red traffic lights, etc.

PROBLEM PROGRAMMING

Such a wonderful convenience is this deeply embedded, virtually essential to survival, auto/self programming function we carry.

> ### YET, WE ARE STARTING TO SEE THAT SOMETHING
> ### IS NOT WORKING WELL.

Deep within ourselves, where we carry this capability to program ourselves, we find this necessary program-ability function of ours is running far afield, seemingly out of control. **Or, and I dare also ask this:**

> Is the addiction pattern program
> actually *in* control,
> seeking ever greater control
> over its hosts—over us?

(And, I do at times also ask this additional question: **Might this programming actually also include programming to** *appear* **to be** *healthy* **programming at times running awry while** *quietly pressing its invasion ever deeper* **into our minds and bodies? I reserve this for another discussion.**[20])

---

[20] I discuss this matter in greater depth in other books. For example, see books in the KEYS TO CONSCIOUSNESS AND SURVIVAL SERIES such as UNVEILING THE HIDDEN INSTINCT and also OVERRIDING THE

And, when this running awry happens, we can almost obediently grow quite detrimentally, even quite dangerously, addicted to using drugs/alcohol, substances, and to other dangerous behaviors more in the nondrug (non-substance) arenas. (These dangerous patterns do also include troubled cognitive and emotional patterns. Let's not overlook how problem addiction patterns can exist on so many levels and take so many forms, including forms playing out well beyond obvious, visible, explicit drug/alcohol/substance addictions.)

These drug and nondrug (behavioral and even emotional) pattern addictions are perilously prevalent these days, and ongoing. It seems we, even with all our well intentioned science and religion and the essential self help and peer practices, have of course neither backed this problem away *nor fully understood what this problem is* (and how far beyond substance addiction this problem reaches—affecting all our lives.)

Of course the problem addiction program is designed to block us from recognizing its nature and presence, from detecting it, from *SEEING ITS HIDDEN FACE*.

Deep within the recesses of our minds, and the biological brains that carry our minds, we find microscopic, even submicroscopic, processes enacting themselves according to our programming, our wiring. While in several other books I discuss consciousness and what consciousness is or might be,[21] here I want to look at the brain's programming for what

---

EXTINCTION SCENARIO. Refer to recommended reading list at the end of this present book, *SEEING THE HIDDEN FACE OF ADDICTION*.
[21] See books listed in the preceding footnote.

it is and for what it does to us. Of course, as the brain IS US (or a key part of us and our consciousness) according to most scientists, then this book does address the consciousness. (Indeed, I do share parts of my *Going Conscious Processes* in later chapters of this book, with our consciousness as a key factor.)

This being said, be on the lookout for the *enslavement* of the person, or of that person's brain, or of that person's mind, or of that person's SELF – enslavement to the problem addiction program/matrix itself.

Biochemical and bioelectric, and other forms of messages less known to us, race through our brains, spilling among our cells, neural pathways, and synapses, directing our choices, actions, feelings, thoughts, and all that relates to these.

It is there, at the most invisible micro level, that our biologies, directed by our programmings, decide whether we will grow addicted and to what we will grow addicted, and what will be the effects of our addictions.

So how free are we, one might want to ask here. Are we free enough to:
(a) choose to or not to be addicted; and to
(b) choose what to be addicted to,
or what not to be addicted to.

Not entirely, not entirely free that is. (Our Free Will itself can be invaded, usurped, controlled by problem addiction programming.)

HERE WE ARE, CONSCIOUSNESS

So here we are again, face to face with what some will tell us is indeed the consciousness, or at least what the *self* thinks is its own consciousness.[22]

Yes we are, to some extent, *what* our biological brain tells us *we* are, *who* our brain tells us *we* are. And we may live there, in that biological brain, right down in there at the submicroscopic level where we are being controlled by our pattern programming functions. Or we may have the option to override what takes place under the radar, deep down in there. We may have the option to override the invasive programming that can work on this level where our *aware* consciousness does not readily go.[23]

Yet, we are not simply what we find there. The persona, the Will, the being, whatever its source, is more than a cellular or electro-biochemical thing. And it is more than a collection of these things. The whole is greater than the sum of its parts. So are we.

WE CAN BE
GESTALTING THE ADDICTIONS

---

[22] See again, *UNVEILING THE HIDDEN INSTINCT* listed in the recommended reading at the end of this present book, *SEEING THE HIDDEN FACE OF ADDICTION.*

[23] Again, refer to the book, *UNVEILING THE HIDDEN INSTINCT,* for my detailed discussion of the *aware consciousness,* the *conscious awareness,* and the *awareness* itself. Also see *OVERRIDING THE EXTINCION SCENARIO, Part One,* where I delve into our brain's (brain system's) inherent programming problems.

We are, whatever we are, more than simply a biological process. And these selves we have, these selves that can run into challenges and problems in living, can speak to us.

When a problem addiction pattern overtakes us, takes control of our *selves*, we can talk to our *selves* and also to the problem addiction patterns dominating them (us). Yes, we can. We can begin to separate ourselves, our Identity, from identifying with, from the control of, the invasive problem addiction patterning program/matrix.

WE CAN SEPARATE FROM OUR PROBLEM PATTERNS.

As I further explain in later chapters of this book, we can call what is influencing us, operating us, driving us, out of the shadows. We can SEE THE HIDDEN FACE OF ADDICTION, we can DETECT AND CONFRONT THIS INVASIVE PRESENCE.

I work with my clients to help understand and detect this invasive presence. I do this with my *Reality/Form Completion Approaches* and *GestaltING Addiction Matrix Processes*. These approaches and processes allow clients to begin to see more of **what is driving addiction-related perceptions and behaviors.**

We can detect and then *differentiate ourselves from* these patterns to find our SELVES in there, behind these patterns of addiction, to allow us to:

unveil our
SELVES
to ourselves.

Part Three

Coming Face to Face
With the Invasive Program

"Addiction, I see you now.
Think you can fool me? Control me? Kill me?
NO, I won't let that happen."

11
Note About
Chapters in Part Three

The following chapters share another level of this *SEEING THE HIDDEN FACE OF ADDICTION* and the *DETECTING AND CONFRONTING of THIS INVASIVE PRESENCE*. Here, work with persons who are being guided in this process of seeing and confronting the invasive presence, the ***problem addiction pattern program matrix***, is described. This involves the *Reality/Form Completion*, the *Going Conscious*, and the *GestaltING Processes* I have developed and shared with many clients, clinicians, counselors, researchers, trainers, and students. This also involves the *Pattern Awareness Concepts* I share in *Chapter 13*. (For a list of some of the *Process Steps* I apply in this work with clients, see the brief charts of *Part Three* chapter contents on the last pages of this chapter, *Chapter 11*.)[24]

Note that while the following chapters were originally written for psychotherapists and clinicians, these chapters are also being read by others including persons seeking to know more about their own problem addiction patterns. These understandings and processes are of course available to all Readers. (Many of my own

---

[24] Another key element in my work is the identification and understanding of *patterns* we form and live by, and how such patterning can dominate us and our behaviors. All who are guided in the *Reality/Form Completion, Going Conscious,* and *GestaltING Processes* I share in these chapters are also guided in the *Pattern Awareness Concepts and Processes* I elaborate upon in another book, *NAVIGATING LIFE'S STUFF*.

clients read this material and tell me that they, "appreciate seeing all this from the therapist's seat, and better yet, from the addiction's seat.")

Readers, no matter what your personal or professional backgrounds, I welcome you to read on. Please note however, that all those who want to work with these principles and processes, *who seek to identify and confront this invader, the problem ADDICTION MATRIX*, are urged not to do this alone, and to seek highly trained professional guidance in working with these simple yet powerful ideas.

Thank you.

NOTE: The brief charts on the following pages offer an overview of the coming chapters where I share an introduction to the Process Steps I apply in SEEING THE HIDDEN FACE OF ADDICTION: DETECTING AND CONFRONTING THIS INVASIVE PRESENCE. Ideally, Readers will scan these charts before reading the following chapters, so as to have an overview of all this before beginning.

PROCESSES AND PROCESS STEPS OVERVIEW CHARTS

CHAPTER 12: Recognizing and Facing the Invasive and Ingrained Problem Addiction Matrix

Chapter Section	Process Step
Responsibility to Learn	
Talk to the Addiction	
	Modeling the Process
	Separating from The Addiction
	Agreeing to Safety Tools
	Giving the Addiction Characteristics
	Seeing the Struggle
	Guiding the Process
	Speaking to The Problem Addiction
Boundaries Matter	
	Seeing and Defining Boundaries
	Seeing and Defining Inner Boundaries
Continue this Work	
We are Not Our Addictions	
Dis-Identifying from The Problem Pattern	
Take Ourselves Back	
Going Conscious is Becoming More and More Aware	
Grow Conscious Of Patternings	

Chapter 12 provides an opening example of the *GestaltING Processes* presented here in *SEEING THE HIDDEN FACE OF ADDICTION.*

CHAPTER 13: Patterning and Pattern Awareness Concepts

Chapter Section		Pattern Awareness
	1)	Four Basic Patterns
	2)	Patterns Can Be Found within Patterns
	3)	Paradox Patterns Can Hold Us Stuck, Trapped
	4)	A Lifetime Can Be Mapped According to Patterns
	5)	Energy Held in Paradox Can Be Carefully, Constructively, And Powerfully Released
	6)	Insight Patterns Can Lead To Elevation Patterns, Elevations in Awareness

Chapter 13 brings in the *Patterning and Pattern Awareness Concepts* I teach clients participating in these *Reality/Form Completion, Going Conscious,* and *GestaltING Processes* introduced in this book. As all addiction behaviors are formed both within and as a result of patterns we form, our increased awareness of our patterning "functions" and "disfunctions" is essential. This *Pattern Awareness* is further explained and detailed in the book on patterning I have written for clients and others to read, NAVIGATING LIFE'S STUFF: SEEING MEANING IN OUR PATTERNS AND PROCESSES. Readers are encouraged to see NAVIGATING LIFE'S STUFF to read more deeply the *Patterning Awareness* material.

CHAPTER 14: Undrugging the Feelings

Chapter Section	Process Step
Unpacking The Overwhelm	
Another Side to Overwhelm	
	Infected Reality/Form Completion
Encountering The Emotions	
Unbundling Emotions	
	Emotion Expression/Release
Reminder Regarding Power Tools	
Call in Pattern Awareness	

Chapter 14 discusses the experience of coming into emotions that have been previously distorted, suppressed, and or blocked by addiction programming effects. This chapter defines and discusses this *Undrugging Experience* and its characteristics.

As the mind/brain emerges out from under the weight of the addiction program matrix, moments of lucid (what some may call "authentic") experience may take place. While this is a positive increase or advance in self awareness, this can be a great deal to take in and process. The old adage, "welcome to reality," is best if restated:

"Welcome to reality, let's learn how to live here."

CHAPTER 15: The Going Conscious Process

Chapter Section	Process Step
Difficult to Distinguish	see next chapters
Retrieval of the SELF	see next chapters
Being Conscious, Yet More Conscious	see next chapters
Making Our Brain's Executive Control and Metacognition Functions Accessible to Everyone	see next chapters
Awareness	see next chapters
Most Importantly Begin by Becoming Aware of Awareness Itself	see next chapters
Going Conscious Beyond Mindfulness	see next chapters

Moving more deeply into the *welcome to reality thinking* expressed on the previous page, I explain to my clients that *Going Conscious, ever more conscious and aware,* is a process that must be navigated with great awareness. (For more detail on this *NAVIGATION* I speak of, see the book where I share more about this process: *NAVIGATING LIFE'S STUFF.*

In the following chapters, the *Going Conscious Process* I teach is exemplified by the successive therapeutic processes and awareness-es described. Therefore, *Chapter 15* defines the *Going Conscious Process* that builds on *Pattern Awareness* and *Reality/Form Completion,* and that builds into *GestaltING Steps.*

CHAPTER 16: GestaltING the Addiction

Chapter Section	Process Step
Differentiating	
Resuming the Addiction in the Chair Process	
	Conceptually Differentiating
	Separating
	Speaking
	Dialoging
	Releasing
	Completing (for now)
	Recognizing Emotional Engagement
	Continuing to Guide Safety
	Closing (for now)

Chapter 16 moves deeply into the *GestaltING Process*, guiding participants in detecting and separating from the addiction pattern program/matrix.

This process is best conducted with the guidance of a highly trained clinician or guide as emerging memories, along with newly undrugged emotions and sensations, and energy shifts and releases, etc., may require care, attention, and adept management in order to avoid confusion and to maximize the benefits of this therapeutic process.

CHAPTER 17: Addiction GestaltING Itself

Chapter Section	Process Step
Clients Who Want to Speak to the Problem Addiction	
	Appreciating Imagination as a Tool
	Allowing Clients to Say When Ready
	Struggling to Separate
	Separating Partially
	Engaging in Communication With the Addiction
	Stopping or Pausing the Process
	Letting the Problem Addiction Matrix Sit in Both Chairs
	Trying to Outwit the Addiction
	Calling on the Group
	Shifting the Locus of the Addiction Further Out
	Sustaining
	Imagining as a Tool
	Visualizing to Form New Neural Pathways, New Learnings, AHAs
	Allowing the Slowest, Most Prolonged, Ongoing AHA for the Most Lasting Change
	Drawing the Matrix to Gestalt Itself: Release from Paradox

Chapter 17 introduces the next level of the *GestaltING Process*. Here, metaphorically (and or actually—Readers, you decide), **Addiction Gestalts ITSELF.**

CHAPTER 18: Seeing the The Presence and Power of Multiple Paradoxes

	Process Step
Seeing How Deeply The Paradox is Planted	(see the GestaltING Processes presented in all these chapters)
Identifying Basic Paradoxical Opportunities	(see the GestaltING Processes presented in all these chapters)

Chapter 18 explains: the *power of Paradox* (see *Chapter 13* for the basic thinking behind this statement); and also, the **power of multiple and compounded** *Paradoxes.*

Paradox offers great opportunity for positive growth when it is understood.

Growing ever more aware of the presence, sensations, and characteristics of *Paradox* is essential. *Paradox* is a pattern where we sense, on some level, the pressing of agendas, of purposes, of energies, against each other, in a trapping sort of situation.

A seeming no easy exit, lose-lose sort of double bind is part of the *Paradox*ical experience problem addiction presents. See *NAVIGATING LIFE'S STUFF* where *Paradox* is discussed in depth.

CHAPTER 19: Navigating the Emotional Terrain in GestaltING

Section Title	Process Step
Conscious Awareness and Involvement of The Mind/Brain	
Walk With Our Clients / With Ourselves	
GestaltING the Addiction Matrix Process Steps	
1)	Consciously Activating The Metacognition
2)	Coming Face to Face with The Invasive Problem Addiction Program/Matrix
3)	Seeing the Matrix as Separate from the Self
4)	Knowing the Space Between The Addiction and the Self
5)	The Matrix GestaltING Itself
6)	Conscious Awareness and Understanding Of the Matrix and Its Workings
The Art of Orchestrating the Transformational Juxtaposition	
SUMMARIZING DIAGRAM	
	TAKE YOURSELF BACK FROM THIS INVASIVE PROBLEM ADDICTION PATTERN PROGRAM

Chapter 19 offers as summary, six progressive *GestaltING Process Levels or Steps* that can, along with the specific *GestaltING Process Steps* described in each of the following chapters, be followed to guide clients and others, including ourselves, in coming face to face with the problem addiction pattern program matrix, in *SEEING THE HIDDEN FACE OF ADDICTION: DETECTING AND CONFRONTING THIS INVASIVE PRESENCE.*

12
Recognizing and Facing
The Invasive and Ingrained
Problem Addiction Matrix

> I faced my future as I stood and stared.
> Then out of the darkness there came
> another image of myself to see
> with features exactly the same as me.
> All at once it became so clear
> my life was really on the line.
> I knew that if I really wanted to live
> I'd have to see my life as mine.
>
> *Anonymous Group Therapy Participant*

Throughout this book, I describe problem addiction as an invasive opportunistic programming, driving parts of our generally functional healthy programming, even the function of our brains, to run far afield, extremely awry.

IMPORTANT NOTE: I strongly recommend and advise that practitioners, psychotherapists, clinicians, counselors, guides, (and others) who utilize these *Reality/Form Completion, Go Conscious,* and *GestaltING Processes* I offer herein, and any other intensive therapy processes, in their work with clients and patients (and others, even themselves) advise clients and patients (and others) up front and at all points during these processes, that this deep work is not a one-time never need look again experience, that there can be long term realizations that surface far later, that this is the beginning of a lifetime of addressing far and deeply reaching issues that must be addressed on an ongoing basis.

RESPONSIBILITY TO LEARN

I have noted, as I do for clients, that my definition of addiction (being an invader, an invasive program, not part of who we truly are) does *not* mean that persons experiencing problem addiction have no responsibility for addressing the problem. Their responsibility is to learn as much about themselves, about who they truly are, and to allow their actual selves to stand up to the invasive problem addiction patterning. **(Problem addiction, I see you, I know what you are doing here. I will work to defeat you, and to become more of WHO I AM AND YOU ARE NOT: MY SELF.)**

TALK TO THE ADDICTION

Whether metaphor or actuality, the mind can work with this concept: This perception of problem addiction speaks to the individual client *as well as to the invasive problem addiction itself.* And, I have felt so very strongly so very many times, that I am speaking yes, to a client experiencing a problem addiction, and then also to that problem addiction matrix itself.

MODELING THE PROCESS

From time to time, I ask a psychotherapy client (a client who says he or she would like to work with this "metaphor") to visualize moving the problem addiction pattern program (this addiction matrix) outside of him or her SELF, over to a chair some distance away from where this client is sitting. I offer to model what might be done, and some clients like this. I motion that I am pulling something out of myself (often from right in front of my heart area, sometimes out of my forehead area) and then actually taking it over to an empty chair somewhere in the room.

SEPARATING FROM THE ADDICTION

Then I return to my chair. Actually, quite often, I go ahead and place my chair over near the problem addiction's chair, so that my chair is facing the problem addiction in its own chair. Then I sit in my chair, facing the problem addiction. I allow my demonstration of this to be humorous if this is received best to begin the process. I begin a conversation, speaking to "my" problem addiction, "I have moved you out of myself to talk to you. Stay where I put you."

AGREEING TO SAFETY TOOLS

Many clients choose to go ahead and give this a try. Before they begin, we agree that I or they can stop the process at any point, just by saying, "I am stopping this now." Or I or we can call a "time out" to pause or entirely stop the process. Once the stopping and time out agreements are made, we begin. Many clients agree that to begin with, they want to treat this, "like a play, and pretend this is acting, not really happening." This proves, for many, to be a safe way to begin.

GIVING THE ADDICTION CHARACTERISTICS

Some clients choose to give this problem addiction pattern (this presence, this problem addiction programming) a face or other "Human" or "animal" characteristic/s. Other clients choose to give this pattern, this problem addiction matrix, some kind of shape or form. Sometimes clients choose to draw or scribble something symbolic of the problem addiction pattern program/matrix and literally take it over to a chair some distance away, and place it there.

SEEING THE STRUGGLE

Of note is how frequently clients act out, either as what they choose to call "a play" or "play acting," or as what they say is something they feel is "really happening right now," a **separation Struggle.** *They report that the problem addiction pattern matrix is fighting with them when* they try to pull it out of themselves. Others say that the problem addiction pattern matrix "keeps trying to get back into me." Some clients choose to act out this Struggle between themselves and the addiction pattern program matrices inhabiting them. This Struggle sometimes continues for several minutes (or longer). Clients know that they can stop or pause the process as they have earlier agreed to the stop and time out tools.

GUIDING THE PROCESS

The psychotherapist guiding this process must remain highly alert at all moments of this process, calling a "time out" or an "I am stopping this now" or a "freeze" whenever safety appears to be an issue. Sometimes, pausing the process and checking in is what is needed. Many clients will want to try this again, and this is acceptable. Ask clients to agree not to conduct this process on their own at this point in their learning, and not to guide others in doing this.

SPEAKING TO THE PROBLEM ADDICTION

Once this imagination and even visualization is working for the client, the client and I speak to this problem addiction pattern program (this addiction matrix). Often, the client describes this problem addiction pattern/matrix, sometimes even describing its characteristics as being those of a living thing, a life form or an intelligence of its own[25] — almost a sentient being, a stubborn one, resisting not only having to stand (sit) outside the client's body, but also **being resistant regarding its being detected, identified, in the first place.**

Dialog begins between the client and this addiction pattern program matrix.

---

[25] Refer to my discussion of this concept in UNVEILING THE HIDDEN INSTINCT.

*At this point in the process, many clients speak to "their" addictions. "I hate you," "leave me alone," "get away from me," "look what you're doing to me," and other statements are made, sometimes shouted or cried. This is the beginning of the clients talking to the addiction program/matrix inhabiting them. This is also the start of the clients <u>**conceptually differentiating themselves**</u> from the addiction pattern program matrix.*

Note:
See *Chapters 16* **and 17 for a continuation of the above process.**

BOUNDARIES MATTER

Many times, clients engaging in this exercise comment that they are having difficulties warding off the matrix in the chair pushing to re-inhabit them, the addiction program/matrix' press to return to their bodies and brains. Here is where a discussion and practice of <u>**defending one's boundaries**</u> is essential.

SEEING AND DEFINING BOUNDARIES

I frequently have clients do what I call the **personal boundary exercise.** *This involves standing or sitting up with room to stretch their arms out in all directions. Clients are asked to draw invisible but very real boundaries around themselves, with those boundaries defined by their hands being out (at arm's length) from their bodies. Years after this exercise, I hear from clients they are still reminding themselves of their personal boundaries by reaching out and defining their personal space as that within arm's length of their bodies.*

SEEING AND DEFINING <u>INNER</u> BOUNDARIES

For those who are ready, we take this exercise out of the physical into the mind, and draw boundaries even around metaphorical cells, or for some even around their **selves** *or* **souls.**

*When working on the processes described on the previous and following pages (the concept of clients moving their problem addiction program matrices out of themselves in order to **identify, differentiate from, and confront** them), **having personal boundaries not only defined but very clear** is quite valuable, even essential. These (conceptual and actual) boundaries between themselves and the invasive problem addiction program matrix can be ever more distinct and strong with time.*

CONTINUE THIS WORK

The exercise (described earlier in this chapter) can be done intensely in a two or three day workshop, or can become a long term process, with some clients coming back to do more work like this regularly, beginning a week or a month or even years later.

I always advise clients that they do best to continue to work, even over the years, on the matters raised during these *Reality/Form Completion, Going Conscious,* and *GestaltING Processes.*

WE ARE NOT
OUR ADDICTIONS

I emphasize to clients experiencing problem addiction patterns that *we are not "our" problem addictions, even when our identities feel (appear) to have been subsumed in varying degrees by these addiction patterns.*

WE ARE <u>NOT</u> WHAT SEEM TO BE OUR ADDICTIONS, <u>NOT</u> WHAT SEEM TO BE OUR ADDICTION PATTERNS.

This is a simple yet key understanding. While on the one hand appearing rather obvious, this clarity can be amplified on all levels of oneself. This helps to begin to truly ***dis-identify,*** *differentiate*, from the invasive problem addiction pattern program and its matrix, its presence.

I invite clients to step up to the challenge, for many the challenge of their lives, to **unravel themselves** from the problem addiction programming whose goal is to overtake them, their Will, their attention selection, decision making, moral judgement, and other (brain) functions.

While problem addiction is not a science fiction-like invasion of us by an off planet life form (as in the film, *Invasion of the Pod People*[26]) the metaphor is valuable. This allows us to see ourselves as invaded by something alien to ourselves, in this case, the invasive problem addiction pattern program matrix.

Furthermore, once the problem addiction pattern programming sets in, *we may become so invaded that we believe we are who we have become after being invaded,* one of the Pod People, or one of the problem addiction program/matrix people. In this sense, problem addiction works somewhat like a retro-virus, in

---

[26] The 2007 science fiction film, *Invasion of the Pod People*, was a remake of an earlier 1956 film, *Invasion of the Body Snatchers*. *Invasion of the Pod People* tells the story of the invasion of a town in California following a meteor shower. The film's lead character then notices that people around her are changing, that they seem not to be themselves any longer. She eventually finds that a race of mind-controlling off planet life forms, Pod People, who grow in large seed pods, have invaded and are invading people's bodies and minds. At one point, the horrified lead character is encouraged by the Pod People to become an *invaded* Pod person (or in the sense of this discussion in SEEING THE HIDDEN FACE OF ADDICTION, to become or become again the invaded "addicted" or "problem pattern addicted" person), to surrender, to come on over to their side, as everything is fine there. The parallels to the invasive problem addiction program/matrix I describe in this book are clear.

that the invading programming or matrix moves into us, its programming becoming part of us, seeming to be becoming us. (See *Chapter 4*, where I further address this matter.[27])

This invasion can make it quite difficult for us to "expel" a problem addiction program matrix, as this gives us the sensation of choosing to <u>expel ourselves from ourselves</u>. This seeming retrovirus seeks to invade even our Identity to make itself ever more difficult to distinguish and extinguish. (Again, the Paradoxical double bind confines us within its no exit trap.)

DIS-IDENTIFYING FROM THE PROBLEM PATTERN

This is where I bring clients to understand (or to consider the possibility) that unravelling, DIS-IDENTIFYING, differentiating themselves from, the problem addiction pattern program/matrix must be done.

> Addiction program, I am not you.
> You reside in me, in my mind and body,
> hiding within me
> as if you are me.
>
> Yet, I see now that you are not me,
> and I am not you.

This is the message we can share with ourselves and with our clients dealing with problem addiction patterns. We and our clients can *conceptually separate ourselves/themselves* from our/their problem patterns to *isolate* these patterns from

---

[27] Also see books in the *KEYS TO CONSCIOUSNESS AND SURVIVAL SERIES*, such as *OVERRIDING THE EXTINCTION SCENARIO* as per reading list at the end of this present book, *SEEING THE HIDDEN FACE OF ADDICTION*.

ourselves/themselves. We/they can do so more and more every day.

TAKE
OUR SELVES BACK

I see the insidious problem addiction patterning as an invasive *and self preserving programming*. As I have noted in earlier chapters, there are times in my psychotherapy office, when I sense, almost see, *the problem pattern in the room,* while I am working with the person this pattern has invaded. This sensation/perception has been a profound and highly informative view of the problem patterning afflicting so many of us.

I have at times silently dialoged with the problem addiction pattern program lurking there. I have actually done so many times, sensed and witnessed the presence of this ADDICTION MATRIX. I have felt that I was coming face to face with a powerful, fierce, and strange, almost foreign, intelligence, one that actively sought to block my discovery, detection, recognition, and confrontation, of its presence. *At first this was odd, uncanny, and I questioned the experience. Yet, as I continued to work with clients experiencing problem patterns, I found this sensation (of a problem matrix being present) appearing again and again. As a metaphor or a format for framing the work I do, this has been quite valuable. I have sensed the power and hegemony of that addiction pattern and its programming, its matrix.*

I feel what my clients are dealing with, what all of us are dealing with as *we are all prone to problem patterning of some form.* I may tell a client I am sensing the presence of this matrix, I may explain this out the gate, or I may wait to do so, or I may never do so. This depends upon the client.

Some clients do want to know my perspective, do want to know what I am thinking and sensing. Some want to hear what I am saying to this matrix, and if so I share this (although I may filter it somewhat).

I get to know this monster, this problem addiction program matrix, seeking to invade humanity where ever it can.

In working with clients who arrive in my office, some arriving after one or more decades of active problem addiction pattern expression, I see how deeply invasive this programming can be. I see that once this problem addiction patterning is so deeply instilled, entrenched, *this programming is <u>itself programmed to RE-program</u> whatever of our brain functions it can partially or completely usurp.* (I have witnessed several of my clients finding that it took them <u>at least two years of sobriety</u>, after ten or more years of drinking and drugging, to feel that their brains were "just now starting to work again," both cognitively and emotionally.)

GOING CONSCIOUS IS BECOMING MORE AND MORE AWARE

Many persons experiencing problem addictions have felt this, have felt the problem addiction pattern program/matrix seeking to preserve itself, and even seeking to expand itself, even to the detriment of its host – of US.

We must seek to differentiate ourselves from problem addiction programming when this programming can harm us, confuse us, disguise as us.

The more aware, THE MORE CONSCIOUS, we can be of what is taking place within us, the more we can have a say in what we think, feel, and do. Hence, *Going Conscious of the presence and* *effects of invasive problem addiction <u>patterning</u>* is key in addressing problem addiction.

GROW CONSCIOUS OF PATTERNINGS

Key in this *Going Conscious Process* is heightening one's awareness of the impact of programming to form and even be trapped in patterns which are too frequently problem patterns.

Sensitizing to one's patterning is essential in addressing the workings of the problem addiction program/matrix. The following chapter introduces this essential *Pattern Awareness*.

13
Patterning and Pattern Awareness Concepts

This brief chapter is included here as these *Pattern Awareness Concepts* are key in SEEING THE HIDDEN FACE OF ADDICTION. All cycles, habits, addictions, whether related to drug/alcohol or to non-drug behavioral, emotional, and other processes, are built upon patterns. Indeed, it is our *program-ability* (referred to in earlier chapters such as *Chapters 3* and *6*) that renders us susceptible to being patterned, subject to patterning processes, even to dangerous ones.

We all carry this patterning capability, our programming to be patterned, and for good reason: this programming to be patterned can be healthy and even life supporting. However, we live at risk of this programming to be patterned rendering us caught in un̲healthy patterns such as problem addictions.

Integral in the *Going Conscious Process* I write of herein is our becoming increasingly aware of our problem addiction programming. This requires our *sensitizing* to the obvious and the hidden (explicit as well as implicit) patterns and sub-patterns, and repeat patterns, we fall into, even at times get caught in or trapped in. Once we are trapped, the *Paradox* of the invasive addiction programming sets in, and holds us, our energy patterns, (seemingly trapped) within it.

In working with clients to develop their *pattern awareness*, I distill the many patterns we experience into the four basic pattern categories I share in this chapter: *Struggle, Paradox, Insight, Elevation*. Elsewhere, I more fully explain these *Patterning and*

Pattern Awareness Concepts I teach as being key in these *Reality/Form Completion, Going Conscious,* and *GestaltING Processes* described herein. See the book, NAVIGATING LIFE'S STUFF: SEEING MEANING IN OUR PROCESSES AND PATTERNS.

In a nutshell, here are these *Patterning and Pattern Awareness Concepts*....

1) FOUR BASIC PATTERNS

We experience various forms of four basic patterns: *Struggle, Paradox, Insight, Elevation.*

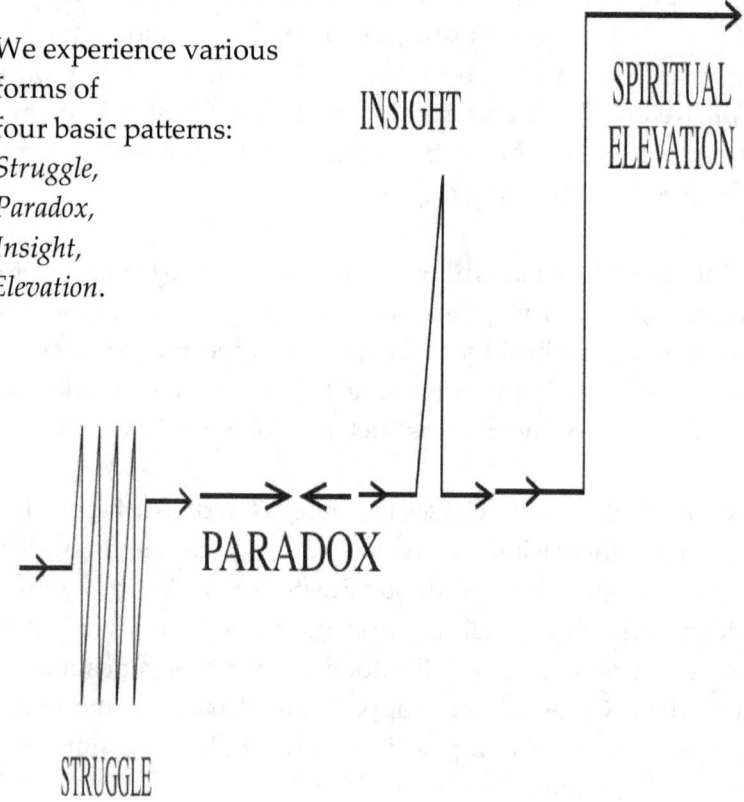

2) PATTERNS CAN BE FOUND WITHIN PATTERNS

Any of the above four basic patterns can be taking place within another pattern, for example, ongoing *Struggle* can be trapped in *Paradox*. (See definition of *Paradox* on the following page.)

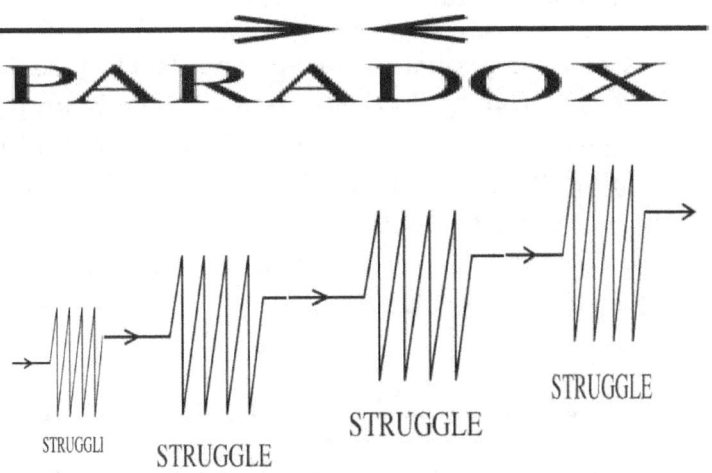

Paradox itself can be trapped in *Paradox*, with multiple *paradoxical situations (or energy lock-ups) profoundly* affecting us while we are unclear what this is. *Paradox* is the lose lose, no way out, no right answer, nothing appears to be an easy option, **double bind** we experience so often. Of course *Paradox* is natural, however when *Paradox* patterns work their way into problem addictions to support those addiction patterns themselves, the trap is set.

3) **PARADOX PATTERN
CAN HOLD US STUCK, TRAPPED**

The *Paradox* pattern is central in any holding pattern, even in the trapping (at times deadly) problem addiction pattern. (*Paradox* is a situation or concept or sensation that combines contradictory characteristics.)

Paradox **is the holding, confining, JUXTAPOSING**[28] **of energies (**<u>*turning of forces and factors against each other ---such as personal survival versus problem pattern survival*</u>**), in a way that holds these energies in a "stuck" pattern or set of patterns. Energy trapped in unhealthy patterns is a *Paradox*ical condition with no easy exit, a lose-lose sort of state.**

As difficult as *Paradox* patterning can be, the adeptly guided *discovery and release* of awareness and energy *out* of the *Paradox* pattern can be profound and positive. As I have often said to my students, *with knowledge of its NAVIGATION, Paradox can be a great therapeutic resource.* (See Point #4 immediately following. See also the book, *NAVIGATING LIFE'S STUFF.*)

---

[28] Note: To *juxtapose* is to deal with concepts and or issues close together to see (or feel) contrasting effects and characteristics. See *Chapters 16,17,18,* and *19.*

4) **ENERGY HELD IN PARADOX CAN BE CAREFULLY, CONSTRUCTIVELY, AND POWERFULLY RELEASED**

Energy trapped in such *Paradox* can be identified and released in constructive ways when this release or *GestaltING Process* (as described in the following chapters) is understood and conducted with awareness. The diagram immediately below indicates that the release from *Paradox* is a release from a trap, from a double binding situation. In this trap are contradicting factors that can be carefully juxtaposed to generate release. See *Chapters 18* and *19*.

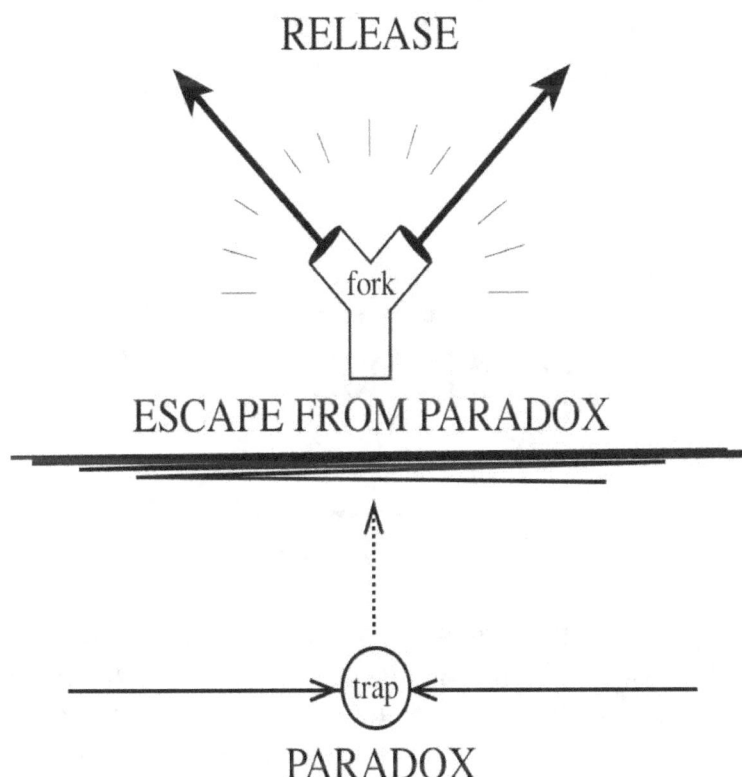

5) A LIFETIME CAN BE MAPPED ACCORDING TO PATTERNS

A lifetime can be mapped according to patterns formed and lived within during that lifetime. There are infinite *pattern sequences and clusters* that may be experienced, and added onto, such as these:

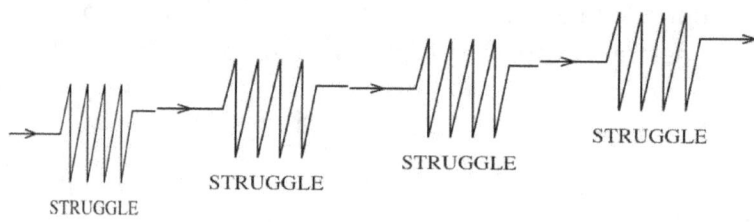

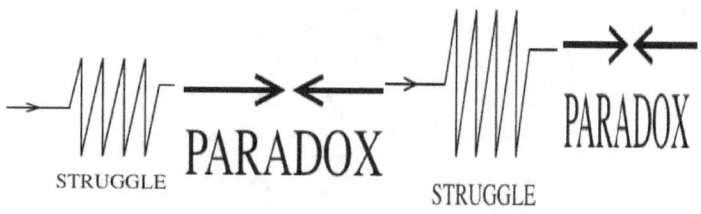

We can map our patterns by linking together the *Struggle, Paradox, Insight,* and *Elevation* patterns in many different ways to portray how we are moving through our lives, even through particular years, months, weeks, days, hours, moments of our lives. (See NAVIGATING LIFE'S STUFF for more on the ***mapping of the patterns and clusters of patterns*** forming passages in one's life.)

6) INSIGHT PATTERNS CAN LEAD TO ELEVATION PATTERNS, ELEVATIONS IN AWARENESS

Where we get stuck or caught in dangerous patterns such as problem addiction-related patterns (these are frequently addiction-related *Struggles*), the *Paradox* of being stuck may be the overarching pattern trapping this energy. Where we catch a glimpse of a way out the problem pattern, this is an *Insight*. Yet, an *Insight* often drops back down into the *Paradox* and or the *Struggle* our *Insight* briefly sees out of.

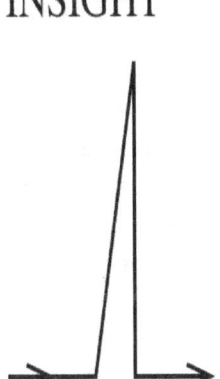

Where we can sustain this *Insight* that breaks us out of the *Paradox* and the *Struggle* it may hold in place, we experience an *Elevation* of our awareness.

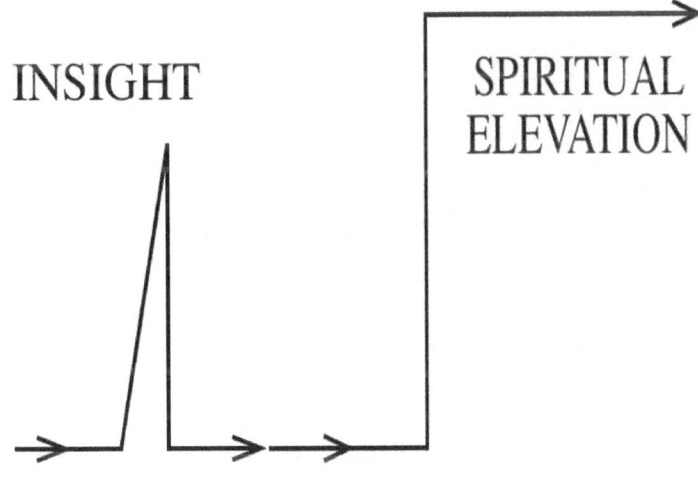

Again note: These ***Patterning and Pattern Awareness Concepts*** presented in this chapter are more fully developed in the book, *NAVIGATING LIFE'S STUFF*.

For the purposes of the *Reality/Form Completion*, the *Going Conscious*, and the *GestaltING Processes* described in the following chapters, this **Pattern Awareness** is central in moving toward the ***realization, confrontation, and release--the GestaltING***--**of the invading matrix, the problem addiction pattern program.**

14
Undrugging The Feelings

The *Going Conscious* I speak of here is like turning on a light. Of course, some lights are on dimmer switches, which means the light will grow progressively as we learn to increase it (or may dim if we don't). We can *go conscious* and see more, and more and more as we continue to go ever more conscious.

The power and potency of our continuously going ever more conscious is great, so great that there may be forces and factors that are driven to suppress this emerging ***aware consciousness***[29] we can generate within ourselves.

As the mind increases its awareness of itself--its conscious focus on its functions such as attention, thought organization, mood management, even impulse control, and other processes--the mind is going *ever more conscious.*

As discussed earlier in this book, *a self preserving and self enhancing problem addiction program/matrix seeks to suppress the power of its host—of us. In so doing, the problem addiction program seeks to <u>(is programmed to)</u> suppress our ability to be conscious (aware) of its presence, and of its actual agenda.*

---

[29] Again see the book, UNVEILING THE HIDDEN INSTINCT, where I define the *aware consciousness,* and include exercises for generating this. See also the book, THE GOING CONSCIOUS PROCESS. These books are listed in the booklist at the end of this present book, SEEING THE HIDDEN FACE OF ADDICTION.

> IMPORTANT NOTE: I strongly recommend and advise that practitioners, psychotherapists, clinicians, counselors, guides, and others who utilize my *Patterning Awareness, Going Conscious, Reality/Form Completion,* and *GestaltING Processes* as introduced herein, and any other intensive therapy processes, in their work with clients and patients advise clients and patients (and any others) up front and at all points during these processes, that this deep work is not a one time never need look again experience, that there can be long term realizations that surface far later, that this is the beginning of a lifetime of addressing far and deeply reaching issues that must be addressed on an ongoing basis.

UNPACKING THE OVERWHELM

Group therapy clients and workshop participants share their experiences and their feelings before and with each other, and discover that they are not alone. They can also learn to listen very closely to themselves and to each other, even to dissect their and others' emotions and problems into manageable parts. I call this **unpacking a problem to see it.** *(Frequently this includes unpacking the overall experience into,* **understanding the overall experience as, patterns and pattern clusters,** *as discussed in Chapter 13.)*

Clients can learn that their own and others' patterns—and their situations, experiences, sensations, perceptions, even emotions, can be unpacked, viewed in segments, considered step by step, bit by bit. This can be learned in group and or individual therapy, or workshop or other experiences.

Psychotherapists, clinicians, and other guides, can learn what it means to **UNPACK THE OVERWHELM,** and how to successfully and safely guide this process. When **UNDRUGGING FEELINGS,** the ***overwhelm itself can be overwhelming.*** In working with clients who are *undrugging themselves* and *unpacking surfacing emotions,* I always make sure to teach my *stop the clock, time out,* and *freeze* functions to everyone so there is always a way to pause or lower the energy, tension, angst when needed. I note that I too may use these tools while working with them. This adds to the perceived safety of the process.

In group therapy, workshop, and other process settings, a shared discovery can take place, a view of the *possibility of manageability* of what at times can appear overwhelmingly impossible to control (such as sensations and emotions playing out in problem addiction and recovery processes). For the individual, this experience of manageability of emotion and then of behavior is a cognitive and an emotional movement toward *increased conscious control* of one's mental and emotional processes, *increased cognitive power,* even what I describe as <u>*meta*cognitive power</u>.[30]

ANOTHER SIDE TO OVERWHELM

There is another side to this story: What we may be overwhelmed by may not be what is actually taking place. Let's back up a minute. ... The brain is constantly completing pictures for us, taking what pieces of the whole of reality it has and completing (estimating, composing, fabricating) the "whole" picture for us.

This means that: any sense we have of what is going on, including any overwhelm we may be feeling in response to what we *believe* is going on around us or within us, is the product of the brain's

---

[30] I have discussed the role of metacognition (awareness and understanding of one's own thought processes) in both learning and personal change in several books. See reading list at the end of this present book, *SEEING THE HIDDEN FACE OF ADDICTION.*

Reality/Form Completion, its visual and other gestalt processing of pieces of our reality to produce our sense of our reality.

So, what is it that is overwhelming us when our *Reality/Form Completion* is happening <u>within a brain inhabited by</u> a problem addiction program? ... Could it be that the <u>infected</u> gestalt, the <u>infected</u> Reality/Form Completion, generates the <u>problem addiction determined picture</u>? Yes.

Recall this diagram offered earlier in this book (pictured below with a new caption added):

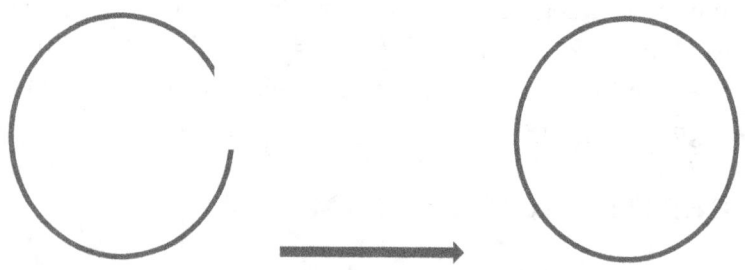

OUR FORM COMPLETION IS
ACTUALLY OUR
REALITY/FORM COMPLETION
Our
perceptions,
cognitions,
emotions, etc.
and responses to these
are formed based on our
REALITY / FORM
COMPLETION/S

<u>REALITY COMPLETION DIAGRAM</u>

INFECTED REALITY/FORM COMPLETION

Here is where we must stop and look again: Could the *infected gestalt*, the infected *Reality/Form Completion*, seek to *fuel* **the sense of overwhelm** so as to hold the individual in, or spill the individual right back into, the problem addiction cycle (Circle **B** pictured on the following page)? Yes. Yes. Yes.

Invading the brain's *Reality/Form Completion* function/s for the purposes of its own agenda, the problem addiction program/matrix infects the healthy perception, decision making, and other functioning of the brain to serve, sustain, the problem addiction pattern program/matrix. ... In so doing, the individual infected by the invasive problem program sees and senses and responds to the world, to triggers, etc., as the problem matrix requires.

ENCOUNTERING THE EMOTIONS

Many persons experiencing problem addictions have long experienced habits/patterns of drugging, burying, blurring, and or distracting themselves from their feelings. Many then manage to experience a substituting of the addiction roller coaster ride for sober reality – for the "real" ups and downs of "real" life.

This is not always a gentle awakening. Frequently, the *Undrugging Experience* drives a return to the problem addiction *trigger sensitivities*, even at times to the urges and cravings that are triggered, even at times to the relapse and or other forms of return to problem patternings.

Running away into, submerging within, the problem addiction patterning can appear to be the solution to stress, anxiety, fear, pain, and other emotions. However, whose solution is this?

Is this the addiction matrix telling the brain this is the preferred behavior? How much Free Will does the person being inhabited by the problem addiction matrix have?

INFECT THE REALITY/FORM COMPLETION PROCESS TO OVERWHELM US, SO AS TO CONTROL US: TO SPILL US BACK INTO THE ADDICTION PATTERN/CYCLE WE ARE CAUGHT IN

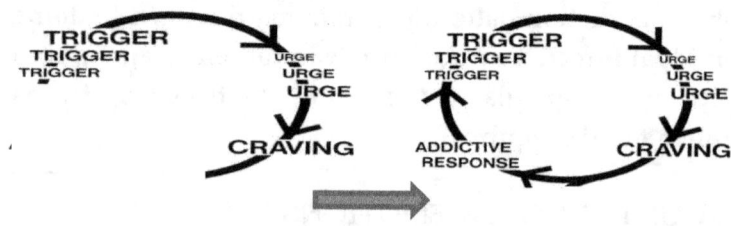

A   B

trigger-to-craving picture of "partial" cycle,
of not using the drug (A)
is completed by addictive response going to "whole" cycle,
of using the drug (B)

THIS (B) IS AN
INFECTED
REALITY/FORM COMPLETION AT WORK
(infected by the problem addiction pattern program)

Circle B = addictive response = relapse or drift toward relapse

ONCE UNDRUGGED

Once undrugged, emotions are frequently far more intensely experienced. So many have described their experience of moving into sobriety as both wonderful and daunting, at times even overwhelming. They frequently report that for the first time in years, and for some the first time in decades, they are "coping with life without the blanket or buffer of drugs and alcohol, or gambling, gaming, or other addictions."

Now actual emotions are being experienced. At times, these emotions can be wonderful. However, many clients describe their *undrugged* experiences facing insecurity, sadness, fear, anger, confusion, frustration, and other emotions as, "So intense I almost wanted to drug myself again," and or, "Too much for me so I went back to drinking and drugging just to cope."

Note that when age at first use of the drug/s (yes, again alcohol is a drug) was in childhood or adolescence, the brain may not have been able to (allowed to) undergo *key developmental phases undrugged*. Hence, the undrugged, unimpeded, **management of emotions** may not have been experienced and fully developed.

Some of my clients tell me they are certain that they are examples of "emotionally arrested development." They express their sense that encountering life unaided by drugs, alcohol, and or the distractions of other addictions such as gambling and gaming, is overwhelming, looks and feels impossible. (Some of these clients began using alcohol/drugs at the age of ten or eleven, or earlier, and then spent their preteen and teenage years, plus their young adult years, and beyond, "under the influence.")

For many of the participants in my individual and group therapy and or workshop sessions, just talking about feelings is a new, or a newly revived, experience. And talking about feelings with the *awareness functions alerted* can be quite an eye opening and challenging experience.

Welcome to reality. Navigating the journey through one's reality may be a challenge for anyone (let alone for those who have drugged themselves with drugs/alcohol or nondrug habits) to manage or even avoid. This is quite understandable, as life is so very challenging. The option to numb or even destroy oneself is offered by the world around us, yes, and also by the invasive problem addiction program/matrix that takes advantage of its host's desire to avoid pain, pressure, sadness, etc.

As a person emerges from the haze of drug/alcohol and or other nondrug addiction, he or she is barraged by a stream of long overlooked (even raw) sensation and emotion. All too often, the simplest of expressions about the simplest of these feelings is a challenge.

FEELING FEELINGS

Feeling "real" feelings, whether perceived as positive or as negative or as neutral, and then talking about these feelings is a skill that may have to be learned or relearned.[31] A group process

---

[31] In the interest of space, this book, SEEING THE HIDDEN FACE OF ADDICTION, does not delve into the material found in the additional companion work I also share with clients, the deep look at our *patterning processes* that I offer in NAVIGATING LIFE'S STUFF. Readers are encouraged to see that book as well. (Note that this *patterning process awareness* is referred to several times in the following chapters, and also most specifically in *Chapter 13*.)

is a good environment for this learning and relearning as there is validation and support in the shared experience process. There is also a safe environment to discover and share emotions that may be surfacing for the first time or the first time in years.

Working with clients as they are *undrugging* themselves requires careful attention, as these clients are experiencing at times new, at times old and stuffed away, emotions with increasing intensity. This requires attention to clients' responses to hitherto "unfelt" (as one client described this), or previously not fully recognized, or not yet managed, emotions. Even *rehearsing the management of emotions* in therapy settings, and doing so many times along the way, is quite useful. (For a basic example, see anger management practices.)

UNBUNDLING EMOTIONS

I frequently keep a chart of faces, hundreds of faces expressing hundreds of emotions, handy. I have been told by clients, "I thought all these emotions were just anger. Now I realize there are many feelings I've been having. Some are anger, some are sadness, some are loneliness, some are frustration, some are shame and other feelings. Yes, there is some happiness in there too, but it gets mixed in with the bad feelings. Like a giant soup."

The tendency to collapse all of one's emotions into one or two general bundles is natural. First, this is a ready response to waves of feelings. Second, emotions that have never been addressed or even defined may have no other label in the mind than a simple grouping into "good or bad feeling," or "happy or sad feeling," or "not mad versus mad feeling." [*And, where the problem addiction program/matrix **infects** the processing of emotions, the emotional jumble can be reduced and deceptively bundled (**infected** in its reality/form completion) into two over simplified categories: "1: not* craving my drug, or my addiction whether drug or nondrug," and "2: craving my drug, or my addiction whether drug or nondrug."]

While we tend to see and even expect the bundling of emotions in very young children, less appreciation for the adult version of this, what I describe as *emotion bundling*, is available (yet is essential).

Back to *unpacking the overwhelm*—clients can learn to safely unpack and manage the bundles of emotion they may be carrying. A safe environment in which to express emotion is first and foremost necessary. Group and or individual therapy (or other) settings can offer this safety.

EMOTION EXPRESSION/RELEASE

As issues that bring forth the expression of emotion are encountered, allow this emotion, encourage it, let it cry or shout or otherwise talk itself out.

*Once there is a pause in this expression, the psychotherapist or guide can begin a gentle directing of re-examining what has been felt in terms of its **bits. Emotions have pieces too.*** *The general and raw expression of raw overwhelm has been invited. Now the expression of pieces of this overall feeling can be invited.*

Consciously identifying and unpacking these bundled emotions can carefully address the <u>overwhelm</u>.

REMINDER
REGARDING POWER TOOLS

Gestalt and other psychotherapy processes conducted with clients as they are *undrugging* their emotions, *undrugging* themselves, can take place short term, prior to recovery, or a short time into recovery, or as an ongoing even lifelong process. Ideally this process is ongoing.

These clients are *downloading*, releasing, expressing, discovering, emotions that are now surfacing, and will continue to surface. More and more, these emotions are being experienced without the filtering and distorting effects of alcohol and drugs and other, nondrug, problem addiction sensations.

The psychotherapist or other clinician or guide must be highly aware of the *undrugging emotions experiences problem addicted clients face*. When engaging in intense and incisive, deep reaching, psychotherapy such as gestalt (or other) therapy can be, the psychotherapist, clinician, or guide does best to move carefully, in steps, checking in with the client at every point along the way to see how deeply and intensively the client wishes to, and actually is ready to, work.

CALL IN PATTERNING AWARENESS

Pauses in the process described in this chapter can bring about both a sense of safety and a heightened awareness of what is taking place, the latter activating the metacognitive awareness.

During a pause in the *GestaltING Process*, participants who are familiar with the *Pattern Awareness Concepts* and *pattern diagrams* explained in *Chapter 13* can practice diagramming their processes and the patterns they see in themselves during this *GestaltING*. **This is a means of drawing <u>conscious attention</u> to what may be otherwise somewhat or entirely under the radar of the conscious awareness.**

15
The Going Conscious Process

I have developed the approach I share in this book according to my view that *problem addiction is an opportunistic and invasive pattern and program, a matrix, a presence, that we can recognize and confront.*

We are all confronted with problem addiction programming, whether or not we think of ourselves as addicted to any thing or behavior or emotion that is seen as unhealthy. We are all wired, programmed, to form patterns of behavior, emotion, perception. And, we are all prone to infection of our healthy programming functions by "viral" problem pattern programs/matrices. So much of this infection takes place out of our awareness.

We must address, even speak to, this problem programming, this dangerous matrix, that is invading our minds/brains, that seeks to control us by infiltrating, working to take control of, our key brain functions such as decision making, moral judgement, attention, impulse control, and more.

> IMPORTANT NOTE: I strongly recommend and advise that practitioners, psychotherapists, clinicians, counselors, guides, and others who utilize these *Patterning Awareness, Going Conscious, Reality/Form Completion,* and *GestaltING Processes* I share herein, and any other intensive therapy processes, in their work with clients and patients (and others) advise clients and patients (and others) up front and at all points during these processes, that this deep work is not a one time never need look again experience, that there can be long term realizations that surface far later, that this is the beginning of a lifetime of addressing far and deeply reaching issues that must be addressed on an ongoing basis.

The *GestaltING Processes* I explain herein can, with informed guidance, lead to progressive increases in awareness of oneself, of one's mind, of one's brain and body. Sensitivity to, and understanding of, sensations previously misinterpreted or overlooked can increase. We can begin to connect with ourselves in new ways. We can become more alert to, sensitive to, the workings of our minds, our brain's executive control functions (ECFs), our metacognitions (processes of thinking about our thinking itself). We can and must always be going ever more conscious.

In that problem addiction programming has invaded the SELF, woven its tendrils into the operation of the brain and body, *even into the Identity*, we are also having to gestalt *our SELVES*—or at least the areas of ourselves (of our minds, brains, bodies, our lives) infected by problem addiction programming.

DIFFICULT TO DISTINGUISH

We may be at the point where we cannot entirely distinguish between ourselves and the problem addiction program matrix that has invaded us (as individuals *and as a species*). This *vague boundary between ourselves and our problem addiction programming* fuels the problem addiction while it is infecting us and seeking ever more control over us.

I strongly suggest that our defense, our strategy to take ourselves back, to strengthen ourselves from further incursion into who we are, is to keenly heighten our awareness, to become EVER MORE CONSCIOUS of what is happening to us, of what is taking place in our minds and brains. We can ever further awaken our awareness to be ever more able to think about our thinking processes. We *can* and must do this, we *can* and must always be *going ever more conscious*.

RETRIEVAL OF THE
SELF

This *Going Conscious Process* I have developed works on many levels of ourselves. This is a conceptual and cognitive, as well as emotional and for many also spiritual, process. This *Going Conscious* is a deeper *discovery* or even *rediscovery* of the self.[32] This is in essence a process of…

> **retrieving the self
> from what has
> occluded, infected,
> invaded the self.
> This invader is the
> problem addiction pattern
> program/matrix.**

The more clarity we have regarding ourselves, who we actually are (and are not—such as: we are *not* our patterns, *not* our problem addiction patterns), the more sensitive to and committed to our actual selves we are, the greater the strength we have to retrieve our SELVES from problem addiction programming—to pull our SELVES out of that invasive problem addiction program/matrix—or better stated, to pull the tendrils of the opportunistic problem addiction matrix out of our SELVES.

---

[32] I offer further discussion of and exercises regarding this matter in these KEYS TO CONSCIOUSNESS AND SURVIVAL SERIES books: *Volume One* titled KEYS TO PERSONAL DISCOVERY and also *Volume Seven*, titled THE GOING CONSCIOUS PROCESS, as well as in *Volume Three* titled UNVEILING THE HIDDEN INSTINCT, all listed in the recommended reading at the end of this present book, SEEING THE HIDDEN FACE OF ADDICTION.

Refining our contact with ourselves is like turning on an internal microscopic scanner. However, we are not looking at biological elements, per se, we are more looking at our sense of our**selves**, our sense of who we actually are,[33] the micro-mini moments of our ongoing existence.

For it is there, under our own radar, below the level of our *aware consciousness*,[34] **that the problem addiction matrix inhabits us.**

BEING CONSCIOUS, YET MORE CONSCIOUS

To allow clients to move closer in to themselves, for example, to have more awareness of what is taking place in their minds and bodies when they are feeling their problem addiction patterning activating/reactivating, I have introduced this *Going Conscious Process* throughout the chapters of this book. Indeed, each of these chapters is an element of the *Going Conscious Process* as well as the *Reality/Form Completion* and *GestaltING Processes*, as these work together. (Note that the *problem Patterning Awareness Concepts* I introduce in *Chapter 13* are key in all these processes, even foundational. See again the book, *NAVIGATING LIFE'S STUFF*.)

Of course, we are all conscious if we are asking ourselves whether or not we are conscious. However, consciousness is a many splendored state. Being conscious of the difference between night and day or hot and cold may not guarantee being conscious of the

---

[33] As noted herein, I further develop this sense of who we are in *UNVEILING THE HIDDEN INSTINCT*.

[34] For definition and deeper discussion of the *aware consciousness*, see books in the *KEYS TO CONSCIOUSNESS AND SURVIVAL SERIES*, such as *UNVEILING THE HIDDEN INSTINCT*.

early indications that one's problem addiction pattern is right there, calling for its activation/reactivation – in obvious trigger-craving ways, yet also in very subtle brain function invasion ways.

**It is heightened and trained awareness of oneself
that can bring greater control
over automatic behaviors and functions.**

**This heightened awareness can generate
increased conscious control
over brain functions such as decision making, attention,
moral judgement, impulse control, and more.**

MAKING OUR BRAIN'S EXECUTIVE CONTROL FUNCTIONS UNDERSTANDABLE AND ACCESSIBLE TO EVERYONE

**The brain's
thought process management system,
<u>the executive control function (ECF)</u>
can be re-owned.
We can reach in and take greater control of our ECF.**

Our ECF generally runs automatically on our un- and subconscious levels. However, I have found that at least some of our ECFs can be consciously put to work to take some degree of control of ourselves, of our brain functions, back from the invasive problem addiction programming. Consciously being more aware of, and then working with, our brain's ECF opens pathways into ourselves that allow for change.

This is going to be what I describe as a *metacognitive process*, a *conscious metacognitive process*.[35] Clients can learn what this process means, what it feels like, what its sensations are, and how to further and consciously activate their metacognitions. *(I delve into this in workshops and therapy sessions, more deeply than on these pages. Note that **metacognition** is "thinking about thinking," being "aware of one's awareness," having an awareness and understanding of one's own thought processes. Also note that the Patterning and Pattern Awareness Concepts detailed in Chapter 13 are additional **keys to activating the metacognition**, as being increasingly aware of one's patterns, even the **subtle patterns and patterns within patterns**, alerts us, and our minds, to what is taking place within **our programming to become patterne**d.)*

AWARENESS

Awareness, while generally present in daily life, is far more than what we tend to think of as awareness (or at least it can be). Awareness is a key element in heightened and empowered consciousness. Again, I note that heightened awareness is our greatest defense against an invasive patterning, an opportunistic program such as the problem drug/alcohol addiction and the problem nondrug addiction matrices.

---

[35] One of my earlier books, LEARNING TO LEARN, and other of my works on *metacognition*, are in essence all about *thinking about thinking*. This leads to my current work on *being aware of one's awareness, of one's thought processes.* For more on *being aware of awareness*, see books where I explain this in depth: NAVIGATING LIFE'S STUFF, also see UNVEILING THE HIDDEN INSTINCT, and THE GOING CONSCIOUS PROCESS, as well as KEYS TO PERSONAL DISCOVERY. See reading list at the end of this present book, SEEING THE HIDDEN FACE OF ADDICTION.

As these terms, *awareness* and *consciousness*, tend to overlap in general usage, let me distinguish between these for purposes of this discussion. We do have a consciousness. This consciousness apparently extends through all of what is called our un-conscious(ness) and our sub-conscious(ness), right up to our *conscious conscious(ness)*. In the latter category, I suggest there are several sub-levels of this level, this *conscious* consciousness.

What I am here calling *conscious consciousness*, is more than simply our daily consciousness: I am somewhat awake, I am relatively alert, I am paying some attention, etc. Certainly we can be and are generally aware we are (somewhat) conscious.

However, having what I describe as an **<u>aware</u> consciousness**[36] or *heightened <u>conscious</u> consciousness* at work is another level, an ever more heightened level, of consciousness. (Note: This is <u>not</u> the "expanded consciousness" that proponents of the use of psychoactive drugs in therapy suggest. This is a *fully conscious*, fully sober, undrugged approach to alerting the mind and brain to as much of its own workings as it can see/sense/know/read.[37])

---

[36] See further discussion of the **<u>aware</u> consciousness** in KEYS TO PERSONAL DISCOVERY and in UNVEILING THE HIDDEN INSTINCT; both these books are listed in recommended reading at the end of this present book, SEEING THE HIDDEN FACE OF ADDICTION.

[37] While SEEING THE HIDDEN FACE OF ADDICTION does not herein take a position on the use of psychoactives in treating psychological conditions and addictions, my intent herein is to make clear that *we must be "unenhanced"* to fully consciously *enhance and empower* our own awareness functions. Our mind/brain is being so very interfered with on so many levels, it is time for us to consciously retrieve ourselves from even what appears to be positively enhancing outside chemical influence.

This this the awareness level I seek to inspire clients to aim for. It is here, in the realm of the *aware* consciousness, that we can "see" (feel, sense, know) ever more of what is going on around and within us, including within our minds/brains. We can detect the presence of the problem addiction pattern program, its well hidden, yet quite obvious once we see it, matrix.

MOST IMPORTANTLY BEGIN BY BECOMING AWARE OF AWARENESS ITSELF

Becoming more and more aware of one's awareness is best done in increments. First, it is important to become **highly aware of awareness itself**, as I demonstrate to my clients by guiding them through this and other processes:[38]

1) To become more directly *aware of your consciousness*, begin with your awareness: grow ever more *aware of your awareness* itself.
2) Take a moment to focus on your awareness. This is *not* about focusing on what you are "aware *of*," such as the person across the room, or the car racing down the street outside your window, or the cake baking in the oven. This is about being *aware of awareness itself.*
3) Sit with your awareness a while. ***Do not be meditating, do not be hypnotized, do not drug yourself.*** This requires a high level of *undrugged and unmediated* alertness. The more awake and aware you are right now, the better. Notice yourself being aware.

---

[38] This and related exercises and processes, I have detailed and explained in these books: UNVEILING THE HIDDEN INSTINCT, and NAVIGATING LIFE'S STUFF, also THE GOING CONSCIOUS PROCESS.

4) Now fine tune your awareness, saying: "Hello awareness, I see you here, being aware of things taking place. Yet now I also see you here, *just being awareness itself.*"
5) Feel yourself **aware of being aware** of nonphysical and non-emotional essences. No need to define these, simply draw your awareness to what else there is to be aware of beyond the first sensations that race in, such as air temperature, hunger, physical desire, etc.
6) This is a **self scan** for levels of knowing and being beyond the explicit obvious emotional and physical realms. *Become increasingly aware of subtle sensations, even seeming flows of energy, and patterns of energy, whatever these seem to be to you.* Do this undrugged. Make notes on this. Do this scan once in a while, making notes on increasing awareness.
7) Track your increasing awareness of sensations you have not been previously aware of, especially those non-physical and non-emotional sensations and awarenesses.

Note: I define awareness as the ***aware and operant*** element of the consciousness. (See UNVEILING THE HIDDEN INSTINCT for a detailed discussion of this.) As simple as is this notion of awareness, this is a powerful resource we have yet to far more fully develop. Our heightened awareness itself will be key in our personal and species survival.[39] Again, this awareness is highly alert and awake, fully and ever more consciously conscious, not meditating, or hypnotized, or drugged in some way.

GOING CONSCIOUS BEYOND MINDFULNESS

A popular teaching quite common in addiction treatment and other fields is the notion of "mindfulness." Mindfulness has been

---

[39] I explain this further in UNVEILING THE HIDDEN INSTINCT and OVERRIDING THE EXTINCTION SCENARIO, *Parts One and Two.*

quite a useful teaching for many, and there is no discounting of this here. Mindfulness teachings include meditation and other similar exercises designed to reduce stress, assist with "healing" processes, and activate compassion, for example.

The *Going Conscious Process* I offer in this (and other of my books[40]) differs significantly from general mindfulness teachings. The *Going Conscious Process* calls for a purposefully highly alert, even metacognitive, and distinctly non-meditative state of mind, calling for a keenly adept and aware state of mind that can sense, detect, confront, even reverse, invasive problem addiction programming.

---

[40] I detail more of my *Going Conscious* work in books where I delve into processes of alerting our mind/brain: NAVIGATING LIFE'S STUFF, and THE GOING CONSCIOUS PROCESS and UNVEILING THE HIDDEN INSTINCT, also OVERRIDING THE EXTINCTION SCENARIO, and KEYS TO PERSONAL DISCOVERY, among other publications.

16
GestaltING the Addiction

> IMPORTANT NOTE:
> I strongly recommend and advise that practitioners, psychotherapists, clinicians, counselors, guides, and others who utilize these *Patterning Awareness, Going Conscious, Reality/Form Completion,* and *GestaltING Processes* I discuss herein, and any other intensive therapy processes, in their work with clients and patients (and others) advise clients and patients (and others) up front and at all points during these processes, that this deep work is not a one time never need look again experience, that there can be long term realizations that surface far later, that this is the beginning of a lifetime of addressing far and deeply reaching issues that must be addressed on an ongoing basis.

Let's return to the description of guiding a client in the ***GestaltING of the Addiction Matrix Process*** (see first part of this description in *Chapter 12* where processes such as *separating from the addiction, giving the addiction characteristics, seeing the Struggle, speaking to the problem addiction,* and *seeing and defining boundaries* are presented as examples). Now, in this present chapter, *Chapter 16*, we move deeper into this process. Here the client is participating in an imagined (or actual, depending on how the client chooses to describe this) *differentiation* between her or him SELF and the problem addiction pattern program/matrix. Here, *Chapter 16* includes processes such as:

      Conceptually Differentiating
      Separating
      Speaking
      Dialoging
      Releasing
      Recognizing Emotional Engagement

DIFFERENTIATING

At this point in the process, the client has already moved to some extent (conceptually, metaphorically, even emotionally) the notion or image or presence of the problem addiction program/matrix out of her or his physical body (out of the SELF) and has "put" this problem addiction in an empty chair.

Note: Some clients report they cannot: "get it to move all the way out of me, it is right here, still hanging on right here." Clients can work with this process in what ever way they feel they can, even if this may require adaptations such as the addiction program being put in the client's hand rather than in a chair several feet away. The psychotherapist continues to monitor to prevent any potential self harm in these processes. Never is a client to use a boffer or even his or her own hand to hit or strike or even threaten his or her own self (or anyone else in the room). No self harm is part of this process.

RESUMING THE ADDICTION IN THE CHAIR PROCESS

Returning to and resuming the earlier (*Chapter 12*) *addiction in the chair* process:

The client is now seated facing this problem addiction. The "dialog" has started, as this section of the process (shared earlier, in *Chapter 12*) indicates:

*[Now] many clients speak to their addictions: "I hate you," "leave me alone," "get away from me," "look what you're doing to me," and other statements are made, sometimes shouted or cried. This is the beginning of clients **talking to their addictions**. This is also the start of their **conceptually differentiating from their addictions**.*

CONCEPTUALLY DIFFERENTIATING

This *differentiating of themselves from their addictions* can be in itself intensely emotional. Clients talk about this process, saying:

"I know this addiction isn't who I am supposed to be, but it's like now, I've gone on like this so long, it's like all I am is an addict," and, *"I am almost afraid to tell my addiction it is not me,"* and asking what becomes a key question:

**"If I let my addiction go, what will be left of me?
It has taken so much of me, of who I am,
can I separate myself from it?"**

?

CAN I SEPARATE FROM MY ADDICTION?

SEPARATING

Once moving further into this ***notion of separation from the invasive addiction programming,*** clients then add to their initial comments, "Wow, this is telling me this might be possible, that someday I will be able take control of my addiction," and "I want to keep practicing this, it helps me see this whole addiction thing differently," and "This gives me some power, a little power for now, and I hope more power over my addiction as this process moves on." As noted in the *Chapter 12* description of this process:

Many clients who choose just to observe others taking part in this process find themselves in tears watching. Some of these observers then want to also be GestaltING their own addictions. Those who proceed with this process move into further communicating with their addictions.

SPEAKING

Confidence builds. Clients are now feeling that they want to try *GestaltING*, or at least speaking to, their addictions:

Clients' communications [with their various addictions] include statements such as, "Addiction, I feel you tugging on me," and, "You are trying to be me," and, "You are getting inside my head, trying to make me follow your orders: trigger, crave, use, trigger crave use, over and over, like you don't want me to escape. **It's like I am your slave.**"

Engagement in the ***GestaltING Process*** grows:

Other clients will choose to move back and forth, sitting first in their own chairs and speaking to their addictions, then sitting in their addictions' chairs and speaking back to themselves in their addictions' voices.

DIALOGING

Moving on from the *Chapter 12* description of this opening to the *GestaltING Process*, the momentum builds. Clients describe and even *voice the dialog* back and forth between themselves and the problem addiction/s they have (imagined that they have, or perhaps actually have, conceptually) moved outside themselves and placed in empty chairs:

> CLIENT: *Addiction, get out of me and stay out.*
>
> ADDICTION: *I will never leave you, I am in control of you.*
>
> CLIENT: *I will fight you for my freedom.*
>
> ADDICTION: *You cannot win. Anytime I want, I can make your cravings so strong you break down.*
>
> CLIENT: *Now that I see you, I know you are not part of me, I can stand up to you.*
>
> ADDICTION: *No you cannot, as I can always take you down. I can even kill you, drive you to kill yourself, overdosing.*
>
> CLIENT: *I will not let you take me down. I see what you are now, you are not part of me, and I can stop you.*

RELEASING

NOTE: *At this point in this particular process being portrayed here, this particular client asks whether he/she might stand up and go over to the addiction and hit it with the padded boffer (padded bat) that had been provided earlier. With permission, the client then does so, and repeatedly hits the "empty chair" where "his/her addiction" is "sitting." This continues for several minutes, while the client shouts and cries and hits his/her addiction.*

COMPLETING
(FOR NOW)

Then the client sits down on the floor in front of the addiction's chair, exhausted, and cries for a while. Everyone in the room remains silent except for their own crying. Several minutes into this, the client stands up, looks at me (the psychotherapist) and says, "The chair is empty now, the addiction seems gone. I don't know where it went, but it is not in the chair or anywhere I can see it, and it is not in me right now. But I will always keep a watch for it, I will always be on the lookout for it trying to take back control."

RECOGNIZING
EMOTIONAL ENGAGEMENT

During the above process, both participating and observing clients are emotionally engaged, sighing, crying, shouting, at times cheering for the client who they see standing up to the addiction pattern program/matrix.

CONTINUING
TO GUIDE SAFETY

During this GestaltING Process, it continues to be the role of the psychotherapist, clinician, and or other guide to monitor for the safety of all participants (and observers) in the room, continuing to offer the earlier referred to (Chapter 12) **stop the process** and **time out** and **freeze options**. Additionally, participants can be asked by the psychotherapist to engage in the **personal boundary exercise** (also in Chapter 12) during a **time out** at any point during this process.

Also, it is essential to continue to remind all participants that nothing can be thrown at anyone, or moved (or gestured, or even verbalized) in a threatening way toward anyone or anything in the room – with the exception of the hitting of an empty chair with the padded bat, and only *if this is approved by the therapist at that particular time.* **Note that the therapist, clinician, or guide will never approve threatening to hit or strike or actually hitting or striking oneself or anyone else in the room.** *Also, no object can be used unless it is a padded bat (or other safe and approved provided object) aimed only at the specific empty chair. Any object being used will be one the participants have already been trained to use and the psychotherapist, clinician, and or guide has already provided and noted can be used and how this can be used.*

CLOSING
(FOR NOW)

Following a client's "work" or "process" such as the one described above, the psychotherapist, clinician, guide, or other facilitator must conduct:

- *A thorough check-in with the particular client who participated in the above process:*
  - *What are you feeling now – first physically – what are you feeling most about your body. (Some facilitators even check pulse and blood pressure at this time.)*
  - *What are you feeling now – emotionally. (Have a list of questions ready to address state of mind, mood, concentration, cravings for addictive behaviors, and so on.)*
  - *What will you be doing the rest of the day or evening, what support systems do you have available, etc. (Have a list of support services and systems such as 800 numbers.)*
- *A review with the client (and all who are present) of what this process was, what took place, its significance.*
- *A check-in with all observers regarding their thoughts on the process and their states of mind and body, and their own support systems.*

- A group and or individual decompression or other relaxation exercise. Following this "clearing," in many instances a repeat of all the above noted check-ins is useful.

- An explanation that this was just a starting introduction to the GestaltING Process, and that there is much more to this work. Those who feel they want to work more along these lines may inform the psychotherapist, clinician, or other guide that they would like to continue. Clients and patients (and other participants) are reminded that this sort of work must be done with a trained psychotherapist as it reaches quite deeply into the SELF, and are also reminded that deep work like this can bring up issues and emotions after they leave. Hence, be ready to see a therapist or clinician as a follow on to this experience.

> IMPORTANT NOTE:
> It is the responsibility of practitioners, psychotherapists, clinicians, guides, and others conducting such processes to inform clients, patients, and other participants that such deep work reaches deeply into the mind and brain, self and soul, and requires expert follow on attention in both the short term and long term.

The material presented in this chapter is but one example of this *GestaltING Process*, and does not address in depth additional portions of the above session or other events. This is simply an excerpt serving as an example of *GestaltING Processes*.

The following chapter continues this example of **GestaltING the Invader**, the invasive programming.

17
Addiction GestaltING Itself

Now let's return to first steps in the *GestaltING Process* introduced in previous chapters of this book. After observing some of this *GestaltING Process* (such as the Differentiating, Separating, Speaking, Dialoging, and Releasing described in the previous chapter)...there may be a next (or the same) client ready to do more of the *GestaltING the Addiction Program/Matrix* work, such as the process steps shared in this present chapter:

> Appreciating Imagination as a Tool
> Allowing Clients to Say When Ready
> Struggling to Separate
> Separating Partially
> Engaging in Communication with The Addiction
> Stopping or Pausing The Process
> Letting The Problem Addiction (Matrix) Sit in Both Chairs
> Trying to Outwit the Addiction
> Calling on the Group
> Shifting the Locus of the Addiction Further Out
> Sustaining Learnings
> Imagining as a Tool
> Visualizing to Form New Neural Pathways and Learnings
> Allowing the Slowest, Most Prolonged, Ongoing AHA
>   For the Most Lasting Change
> Drawing the Matrix to Gestalt Itself:
>   Seeing the Release from Paradox

The following example describes a similar process, this one where the client was guided to *reality/form complete* to detect, identify, the invasive programming, then was guided into a somewhat different level of this work, to have "her" **addiction gestalt *itself*.**

> NOTE: The psychotherapist, as I do, can model for clients these *Reality/Form Completion* and *GestaltING Processes*, demonstrate the various levels and intensities of these processes. This modeling can help set the agenda for a next phase of a therapy process, can open doors to *Reality/Form Completion* and *GestaltING Processes* that may be logical next steps. However, clients should not be required to participate in any process. In other words, never require or demand (or allow peers or group members to demand) that clients participate.

The problem addiction pattern's program/matrix seeks to dominate its host–US–to our detriment. Whether or not this program/matrix has a conscious "mind" of its own,[41] there is an agenda being implemented by this program/matrix, which is to work its way into, utilize, our brain functions in order to operate and control us.

CLIENTS WHO WANT TO SPEAK TO THE PROBLEM ADDICTION

Clients who want to speak to this problem addiction program/matrix with its agenda that is so dangerous for us can do this (guided by a highly trained psychotherapist, clinician, or

---

[41] I discuss further the notion that a program/matrix may have some form of organizational factor, or what I describe as a *systemic intelligence*, in other books such as *UNVEILING THE HIDDEN INSTINCT* and *OVERRIDING THE EXTINCTION SCENARIO*.

other guide) as was described in the previous chapter, first by differentiating then separating from the problem pattern. This is essential as this problem pattern program/matrix has worked its way so very deeply into persons experiencing problem addiction that it has *woven itself into their own identities*. This attempted (or actual) take over *can be confronted and even reversed*, with great awareness.

What does it take to have this problem addiction matrix step out of the shadows, reveal its presence, its invasive program, to us? What does it take to have this insidious problem addiction matrix speak up, actually directly speak to us?

We can work *in terms of metaphor* to engage in this awareness, to open our minds to this awareness. We have seen, in previous chapters, an opening experience, an opening *Gestalt Processing*, of this communication with one's addiction. This is in itself a **conceptual leap** for many participants. This is an initial **Reality/Form Completion** (to detect, identify) and then a **GestaltING** (to differentiate then separate from and confront) this problem addiction program matrix/presence.

***

Now let's take a look at some of the next phases of this *GestaltING* Process....

APPRECIATING IMAGINATION AS A TOOL

I explain to clients that, in order to work with ourselves and the addiction pattern program/matrix, we can give the addiction we are speaking to whatever imagined characteristics we choose (such as a face or voice or body or symbol, or all of these).

The imagination can offer us creative ways of addressing challenges, challenges such as addressing the intertwining of the problem addiction program/matrix with our otherwise

functional brain, and its executive control function / ECF, and other neural functions and processes. It is this intertwining by this invasive problem addiction programming that can harm us, even kill us.

ALLOWING CLIENTS TO SAY WHEN READY

Some observing clients respond that they have now quietly, internally, started speaking to their own invasive problem addiction patterns' programs/matrices. These clients say that they have indeed given these patterns, and these patterns' programmings, voices to help think about dialoging with them. Many say they have already moved at least somewhat into the sort of GestaltING Process described in this and previous chapters.

Some say they are ready to "give this a try and do this aloud." They proceed with the first few steps in the GestaltING Process noted in previous chapters: differentiating, then separating. ... And then, as some of them begin to move more deeply into this process, something happens....

STRUGGLING TO SEPARATE

*For example, one particular client reports that the differentiation has started out as an **imaginary distinguishing** of the self from the problem addiction, but then something has not worked as she had thought it would:*

*She says there has been an unexpectedly intense **separation Struggle**, with the problem addiction pattern **fighting the separation so intensely** that she is tiring simply trying to carry on this separation.*

The client is squirming and clenching her fists. Observers note this and ask if she is alright. She says yes, "But I am fighting this addiction, I have to, I want to, because it won't let me take it out of myself – and I don't want it inside me, inside my brain, running me without my permission, any longer."

At several points during this process, I ask the client if she wants to continue, and or wants to use any particular safety tools (such as the time out, freeze, pause, or deep breathing tools, or the boundary fortifying exercise, etc.). She says, "Thank you, no, I'm OK, I want to do this just this way for now, but I'm so glad I know these tools."

SEPARATING PARTIALLY

The client agrees to move what she can of the addiction into an empty chair, and to then sit in her chair facing this addiction – while knowing that this addiction is still also inhabiting her as the separation process has not completed.

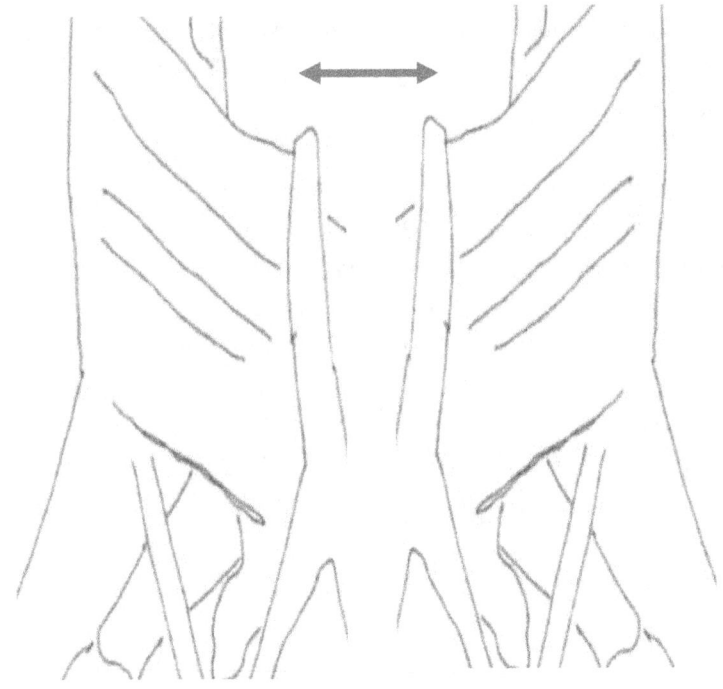

CHAIR TO CHAIR

ENGAGING IN COMMUNICATION WITH THE ADDICTION

Now it is time for the next steps in this GestaltING Process: speaking to and dialoging with the addiction pattern program.

The client in her chair speaks to the addiction program/matrix in its chair: "I can't get you all the way out of me. You have no right to stay in me if I want you out. Why are you still in me?"

The client moves to the addiction's chair and responds, "Because, you fool, I am you. You cannot separate yourself from me."

The client assertively moves back to her own chair to respond, but begins to waver in her certainty that she knows what she wants to say. In this moment, there is a shift in the client's body posture and language. Now the client looks confused and angry as she sits in her own chair and speaks in the addiction's voice:

"Hah, I have you now, you fool! I am sitting in both these chairs. You cannot separate from me." The client's demeanor changes. She is suddenly horrified the addiction is speaking from within her. She is crying, yet says to the psychotherapist (to me), "I can do this. I am OK. I want to keep going with this a while. I will stop if it gets too scary for me."

Still upset, the client quickly moves to the addiction's chair, and says, "Well then, I will talk to you from over here. You are in my chair, so I am in yours." Then the client quickly moves back and forth between the two chairs. She begins to move more and more rapidly, continuing to dialog back and forth.

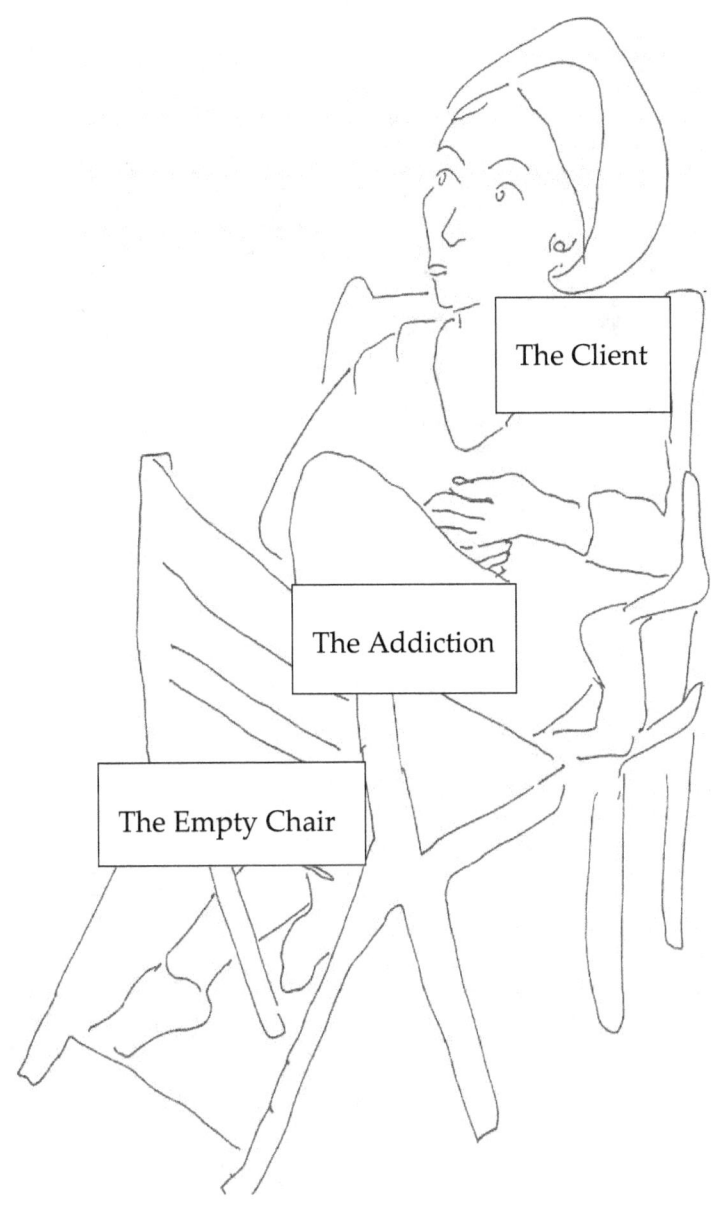

**THE CLIENT, THE ADDICTION,
AND
THE "EMPTY" CHAIR**

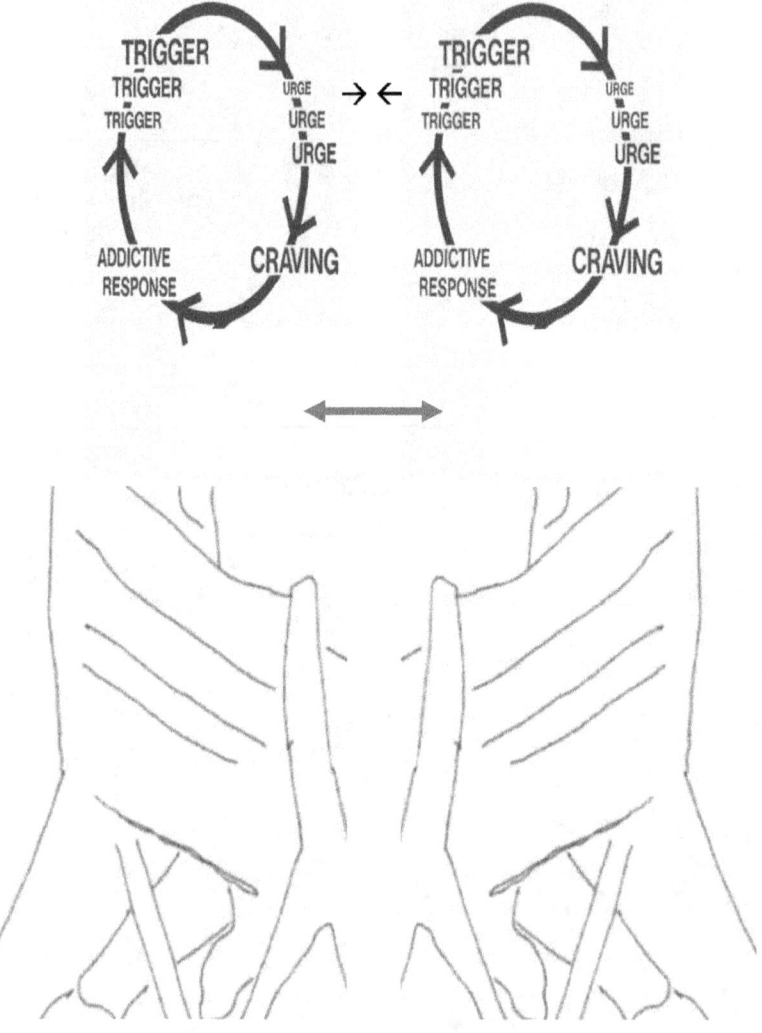

ADDICTION MATRIX TO ADDICTION MATRIX #1

LETTING THE PROBLEM ADDICTION MATRIX SIT IN BOTH CHAIRS

After several minutes of deep breathing, the client says she is ready to continue, that she wants to try to get deeply into the **addiction GestaltING itself** *process. She says she wants to hear what this is again. I respond, "ONLY IF YOU WANT TO AND FEEL READY TO, then* **let the problem addiction program matrix sit in both chairs and call itself out, talk to itself, gestalt itself.***" She says she is "a little scared" but will, if she feels these are needed, use the* **stop the process** *and* **time out** *and* **freeze tools** *that she learned along with this group (the group who is in the room, observing at this time).*

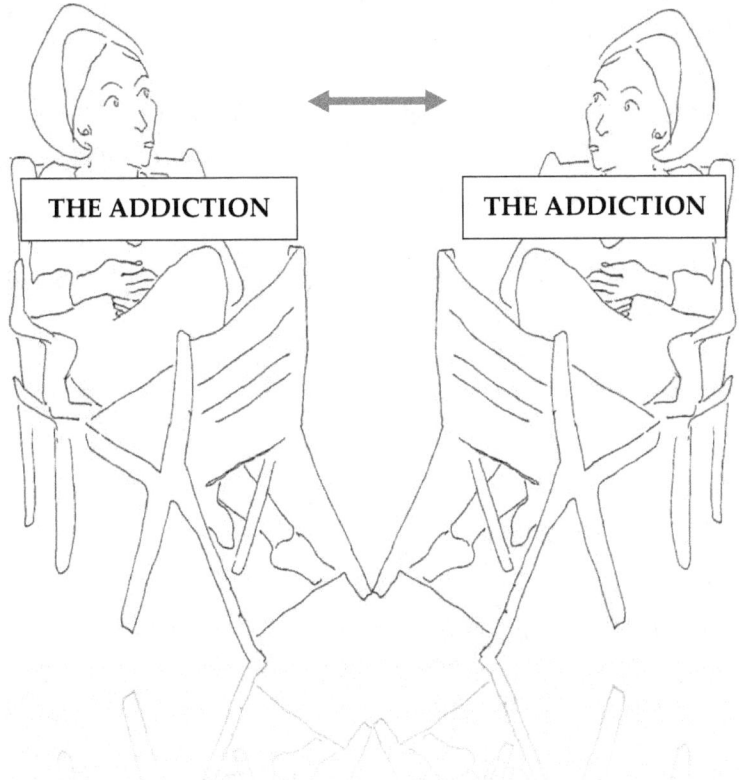

ADDICTION MATRIX TO ADDICTION MATRIX #2

TRYING TO OUTWIT THE ADDICTION

"I am your addiction," the client says to herself aloud from her own chair, still sounding somewhat confused yet determined to proceed. Then, she moves over and says back to herself from the addiction's chair, "And I am your addiction, too. Everywhere you look, I will be there, you cannot get away."

The client moans. She does some deep breathing as she moves back to the other chair. But then she stops. She moves the two chairs closer together, still facing each other, but now just a foot apart.

Now she sits in the chair that had been the "other chair." "You are killing this woman." Then she shifts to the other chair, the one that had been her own, quickly answering, "No, *we* are killing her."

Now the client moves rapidly, almost leaping back and forth from chair to chair, saying:

"No *you* are."

"No *you* are."

"Stop this, get out of yourself, get out of *me*."

"Can't do that, can't get yourself out of yourself, can you?"

CALLING ON THE GROUP

Puzzled and agitated, the client breaks "out of role" and asks the group, "What do you guys think, what should I do?"

Several group members stand up, come over and hug her. They ask if they can sit on the floor near her. She says yes. She continues with the dialog between the addiction program inhabiting her and what appears to also be this addiction program answering back.

"Those people can't help you, they are addicts, too. You can't help yourself no matter what you do," the addiction matrix (the client) says to herself, now sobbing. She moves to the other chair and cries for a minute.

Then she turns to the group members sitting near her and says, "I'm in trouble. This addiction is both in me and outside of me. **It is talking through me to itself.** I can feel that this is not me talking to it. I am trying to get these two things out of here, but they don't want to leave. I can't get out of this right now."

Now I, the psychotherapist, gesture to my colleague who is sitting among the observers.[42] He nods at me, signaling to me he is ready to do as he and I have planned in advance, and stands. Then he says to the client who has been moving back and forth between the two chairs, "Wait." Then he turns to me and asks me, "Dr., can I participate in this client's process?" I say yes, with her permission. He then asks the client, "May I come up and participate in your process?" She says yes.

SHIFTING THE
LOCUS OF THE ADDICTION FURTHER OUT

He proceeds. "OK, look. Your addiction has taken over both chairs. Will you stay here while I carry these two chairs outside?"

"Yes," she responds. She stands still and silent while this is done. (Later she described this moment as "a time lasting longer than it really did, a time when I felt hollowed out, empty, like someone just robbed me of

---

[42] This colleague has worked with me in several of my recent *GestaltING Addiction Group Processes*, and has practiced this next step with me several times.

something. At first I felt like he was taking *me* out of the room with the chairs, and I wanted to follow him, but I did not.")

When my colleague has moved the two chairs outside, he returns without the chairs and stands silently, facing the client. She stands there facing him, also silently, for a few minutes.

*Then the client almost shouts, "Oh wow. I get it. I wasn't in those chairs you took out of the room. I am **not** those chairs and **not** the addiction that was in those chairs. The addiction had been talking to **itself**, not to me. I felt at first like you were taking something away from me when you took those two chairs out. It was like you were taking me away from me. It was weird, I felt robbed, empty. It took a few minutes to bring myself into myself without the addiction there."*

"Yes."

"You moved the two chairs that my addiction was inhabiting out of the room, and I am still in here, standing here alone without them. Thank you. They are not me." Now the client shouts with joy, "Yeah!" and the observers applaud. She says, "Wow, this feels good. Can this stay with me?"

SUSTAINING

*My colleague and I discuss with the group the concept of **sustaining** (holding on to, **Elevating**) **Insight**. (This was learned and practiced in the Patterning and Pattern Awareness Workshops I conducted for clients.* [43] *This group has thus already, in previous workshops and sessions not reviewed in this book, learned about the four basic stages of*

---

[43] See again *Chapter 13* for the four basic patterns (including the *Insight* and *Elevation* patterns) clients are taught, as well as the therapeutic role of (a) *Paradox* release, and (b) *Insight* in awareness *Elevation*.

the journey: Struggle, Paradox, Insight, Elevation, which are diagrammed in Chapter 13. So this group is familiar with the concept of sustaining an Insight in an Elevation of awareness, and what this means in their lives.)

The client comes up and works with me and my colleague to map on the chalkboard the emotional process she feels she just went through. (Again see Chapter 13 and also NAVIGATING LIFE'S STUFF for this mapping process.) The symbols for **Struggle Paradox Insight Elevation** are all used. This allows the client to gain a **metacognitive awareness** of her process: her ECF (executive control function) is drawn into her conscious awareness. This also gives her terminology to explain her process to the group. The group members are (and have already been) asked to make notes on (and map) their own journeys as they watch this client's process.

IMAGINING AS A TOOL

I explain to clients that imagination is a process of exploring ideas, concepts, possibilities, and **developing new neural pathways in the brain, new perceptual processing. Imagination uses creativity functions of the mind and brain.**

I add that visualization is part of this creative process. (I tell clients how I was once affected by a neurological condition which I decided required that I visualize rewiring myself with new pathways for neural messages to travel within and throughout my brain and body. I succeeded in either developing or repairing pathways that messages could travel. I had either imagined that this had happened or it actually had happened. Either way, I succeeded in helping myself.)

VISUALIZING TO FORM NEW NEURAL PATHWAYS, NEW LEARNINGS, SUSTAINED AHAs

The clients discuss with each other the concept that the mind and brain can imagine/visualize moving the problem pattern program/matrix to a place outside the brain and body. I note that this can allow the SELF to engage its brain's ECF, to gain greater **conscious awareness** of the process, to be further **Going Conscious.**

I add that this has been a first process of speaking to the mind and brain, of taking some degree of **conscious control of what is going on under the radar in there, deep in the sub- and un- conscious realms.**

I also note that in this process, the client who had done this with her problem addiction, had placed it in one chair, and then found it within herself in the other chair. Then, she had had the addiction speak to itself – speak from the open chair to itself within her in the other (seemingly also open) chair.

I explain that: Simply by engaging in this imaginary or actual process, this addiction has been GestaltING itself, and thus revealing itself. Were there no addiction to be GestaltING itself, this would be a far easier process. There would be no Struggle, no resistance, as there would be no addiction pattern program/matrix to symbolically or actually **distance from or pull out of the self.**

I add that: when my colleague had taken the addiction out of the room by removing **both** chairs, the imaginary or actual exit of the addiction (matrix) had been further gestalted. I note that this takes place on both the conscious level and on the sub- and perhaps even un- conscious levels. All levels (or many levels) of the SELF feel this, are aware of this.

And the client, well, she had been left behind with her <u>**SELF**</u>. This <u>**SELF**</u> was <u>not</u> the addiction, <u>not</u> the addiction matrix, this was the <u>actual</u> <u>**SELF**</u> free of (or, as free of as possible at that time) the addiction that had been in the chair and in the SELF, in <u>her</u> <u>**SELF.**</u>

"Can this mean I'm free now?" The client asks me and the group.

I respond, "What do you think, how do you want to explain this to yourself? After all, this is happening in your own mind, so the way you process this is up to you."

"I want this sort of thing to work for me. I am committing to continue working this way, gaining more and more conscious control of what is going on inside my mind."

ALLOWING THE SLOWEST, MOST PROLONGED, ONGOING AHA FOR THE MOST LASTING CHANGE

I explain, "To make this work, doing this exercise again and again until it becomes part of your neural memory, an actual **Elevation in awareness**, *is a good idea. Ideally, the first many times, you do this with guidance, with a trained psychotherapist or guide to be present for you as you do this." (I show clients the Insight and Elevation patterns we have earlier discussed. See Chapter 13.)*

At this point, several other group members want to arrange their chairs and take part in the process of having their addictions be GestaltING themselves.

Again, these processes are engaging, and many who at first choose to just observe then gain interest and confidence and want to engage in these GestaltING the Addiction Matrix Processes for themselves.

DRAWING THE MATRIX TO GESTALT ITSELF: SEEING THE RELEASE FROM PARADOX

I have found that: these addiction matrices can seek to do this as well; they will in essence *gestalt themselves* **if brought to this. They actually may seek to** *gestalt themselves.* **This is likely imaginary or actual from the perspective of the brain cells and synapses participating in the gestalt. Or is it? This is up to us,**

the portion of ourselves who are free to force via *Paradox* our addictions to gestalt themselves.

I share with clients this Paradox pattern release diagram they have previously discussed with me, as in Chapter 13, noting now: **What a *Paradox* even this *Paradox*ical gestalt (gestalt of the energy trapped in this very *Paradox*) can be....**

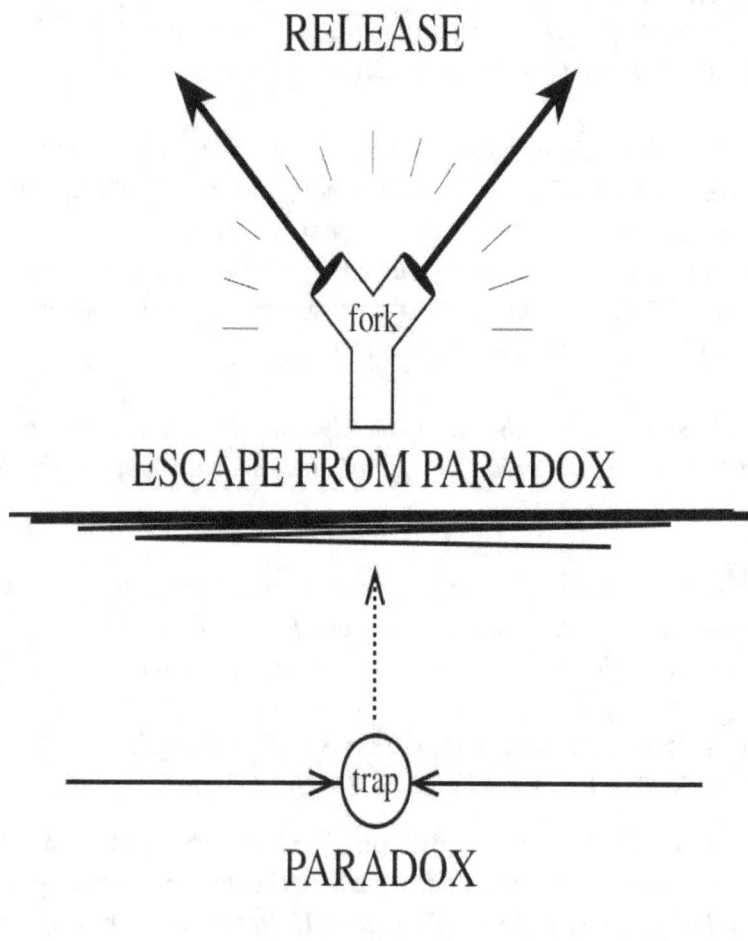

ESCAPE FROM PARADOX

18
Seeing The Presence and Power Of Multiple Paradoxes

The basic and powerful *Paradox inherent in problem addiction* is right here before us: The problem addiction pattern program/matrix functions by using, by invading and usurping, its *host* (US), and our brain functions (US) — all to serve itself.

This powerful yet insidious and obscure process is indeed an invasion of us by this addiction matrix which *disguises itself, its functions, so that they feel to us (to our brains) to be part of us — to be US.*

The sense of being trapped in the problem addiction program is real, as it is this program's purpose to trap us so powerfully that when we try to leave that problem addiction pattern, this addiction program/matrix hits back with heightened trigger sensitivities, urges, cravings, relapse behaviors.

SEEING HOW DEEPLY THE PARADOX IS PLANTED

The *PARADOX* is thus so deeply implanted into us that:

1) By the time we are aware that the problem addiction pattern program/matrix is ever more negatively affecting us, the problem addiction has become explicit enough for us to notice its problematic effect on us, our bodies, minds, lives. The *PARADOX* itself, even if not consciously apparent to us, is being felt, experienced on a deep psychological, spiritual, and biological level.

2) By the time we are aware of the problem addiction, we have already been invaded, and our brain functions to some degree already commandeered by the invasive problem addiction program/matrix. The *PARADOX* itself is in the invasion, as this has been taking place largely under our conscious radar. Even to this day, we (all of us) tend not to realize how invaded we are by problem programming.

3) We may not fully see or sense the reality of this invasion, yet we are invaded, inhabited by this problem matrix. And now, we are the *host* of this problem matrix. The *PARADOX* itself agitates us, makes us feel disturbed, even sick. Yet we still do not see how invaded we are by this opportunistic matrix.

4) This problem matrix has worked its way so deeply into us that at times, stopping or killing this invader feels to be killing ourselves. The *PARADOX* itself is that we have been made to feel we are one with this invasive matrix, that killing it feels much like killing ourselves.

5) This problem matrix even works its way into our own Identity, feels in some way to us to be part of who we are, or all of who we are. The *boundary* between ourselves, our Identity, and this matrix is unclear, weakened, compromised, eroded, invaded. The *PARADOX* itself is this **dangerous boundary confusion.**

IDENTIFYING BASIC PARADOXICAL OPPORTUNTIES

As we increasingly sensitize to, become highly aware of, the *Paradoxes* we are caught in, living with and within, trapped in, we can learn the subtle yet powerful effects of **PARADOX REALIZATION AND PARADOX RELEASE**. This is best done by experiencing this *realization and release* during the *GestaltING Processes* described in these chapters.

We can also sensitize to the *existence of multiple, concurrent, even interacting, overlapping, PARADOXES*. Indeed, there is distinct *synergistic power* in the *multiple Paradoxes* present and at play in the **Addiction GestaltING Itself Process**es described in *Chapter 17*.

With guidance, participants in these processes can sense and utilize the energy caught in the *Paradox* (and *ParadoxES—traps within traps within traps*) so inherent in the problem addiction matrix. Participants can be guided to release themselves (in steps) from the *grasp of this problem addiction matrix.*

The moving of energy trapped in the double bind, the *Paradox*, can be a positive experience, one producing not only great moments of *Insight*, but profound and lasting *Elevations* in awareness. This *realization and release* can be triggered by careful identification of, and then mobilization of, the juxtapositioning energies/factors including:

- the "empty" chair and the client in the other chair.
- the "empty chair" not being empty.
- the addiction resisting being identified, differentiated, separated, versus its strong voice.
- the addiction and the SELF.
- the addiction as part of the SELF versus it not being such.
- the client's role in the process of facilitating addiction's *GestaltING of itself.*
- the addiction speaking to itself.
- and more.

Listed above are just some of the multiple levels of the Paradoxical *juxta*-positioning of factors that can be guided *to catalyze, to gestalt,* areas of the executive control function into the aware conscious level, *to catalyze release from the insidious double bind of the invasive problem addiction pattern program.*

19
Navigating the Emotional Terrain In GestaltING

Everything shared in these chapters is just a start, just a brief look at the *Patterning Awareness Concepts*, and the *Reality/Form Completion,* the *Going Conscious,* and the *GestaltING Processes* that have taken me and many of my clients on such profound journeys into the land of the SELF, and the mind, heart, and soul.

Nothing about these processes I have developed in working with so many clients over the years, brief examples of which are shared in the previous chapters, is meant to minimize, fictionalize, or take lightly these processes of SEEING THE HIDDEN FACE OF ADDICTION and IDENTIFYING AND CONFRONTING THIS INVASIVE PRESENCE.

There is nothing inconsequential or trivial about putting oneself, one's SELF, in a chair, and then putting the addiction pattern/program/matrix invading oneself, invading one's SELF, in a chair *outside* oneself, outside one's SELF, and speaking to it. One's SELF speaking to what is invading one's SELF is a powerful metaphor, a powerful process. For here, in this very process, the invader has been called out, identified:

YOU ARE NOT ME.
YOU ARE NOT PART OF ME.
I SEE YOU HERE,
AND I DRAW (CLARIFY) MY BOUNDARY
BETWEEN MYSELF AND YOUR MATRIX.

In this process, the *creative imagination* is engaged as a tool in the work of: consciously developing *Insight* and then lasting *Insight* or learning (the lasting learning in itself being *Elevation*); consciously engaging with the brain's ECF (executive control function); and, consciously directing some emotional, cognitive, and behavioral *Insight* and change (change being *Elevation* of *Insight* into lasting change in one's SELF, as per the pattern concepts defined in *Chapter 13*):

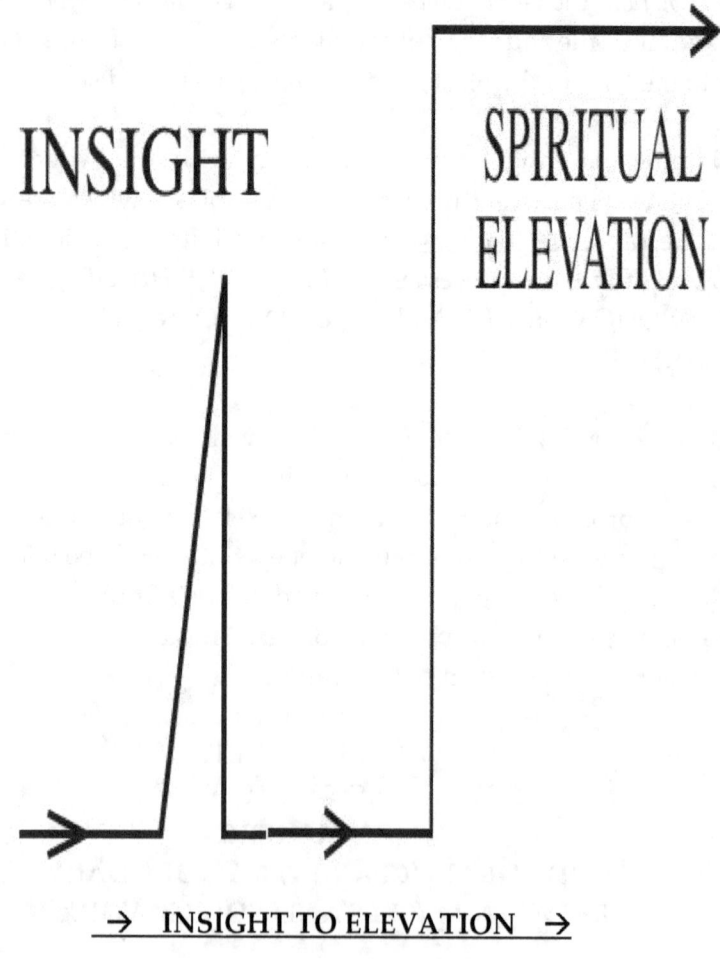

→ INSIGHT TO ELEVATION →

CONSCIOUS AWARENESS AND INVOLVEMENT OF THE MIND/BRAIN

Here is where the *mind/brain can gain conscious involvement in generating new options for itself.* These new options may take practice: require repeated experiences designed to train and retrain us, our brains, to develop new responses; and, engage our brains' executive control functions, their command control efforts, in taking us back, unraveling us, from the invasive problem addiction program/matrix.

WALK WITH OUR CLIENTS/WITH OURSELVES

I suggest that we psychotherapists and guides can "walk" with our clients, guide our clients, as they move deeper into them**selves**, to a place where they can face, even confront, the problem addiction patterns, programs, matrices, that are inhabiting them.

In *GestaltING* these patterns/programs/matrices:

Places within the subconscious where the roots of one's Identity live can be called into the aware conscious realm. A conscious realignment of Identity of SELF can be undertaken. This is not a brief or simple overnight process. This is the matter of identifying, and then unraveling from what is identified: an unwanted presence, a pattern/program/matrix that is weaving its way deep into the subconscious realm, even into the Identity.

In the words of a client engaged in these *GestaltING Processes*, "Now that I get it, I see what is going on. Now I can tell the invasive addiction pattern program that it can no longer inhabit me." (Refer to *Chapter 5* regarding addiction *inhabiting* us.)

GESTALTING
THE ADDICTION MATRIX:
PROCESS SUMMARY STEPS

This seeing, facing, confronting addiction is not only conceivable, this is something that can be done in the therapeutic *GestaltING the Addiction Matrix Process Summary Steps* (**GAMPS**) I have developed for training purposes:

**GAMPS STEP ONE—
CONSCIOUSLY ACTIVATING THE METACOGNITION:**
We are now **consciously activating the metacognition**, the thinking about thinking option of our mind's executive control function (ECF). This is where we can turn a *conscious eye* on the workings of, and pattern infections being conducted by, the invasive problem pattern addiction program/matrix.

**GAMPS STEP TWO—
COMING FACE TO FACE WITH THE INVASIVE
PROBLEM ADDICTION PROGRAM/MATRIX:**
Coming face to face with the invasive problem addiction program/matrix is both *Paradox*ical and pivotal in itself. Simply being able to go to such an (imaginary or actual) locus in time and space, is already a major step. Here is the place in the SELF where the rubber meets the road, where the SELF (realizes, detects, and) confronts the addiction that has invaded it, is now masquerading as part of the SELF itself.

**GAMPS STEP THREE—
SEEING THE MATRIX
AS SEPARATE FROM THE SELF:**
Once coming face to face with the problem addiction pattern program, **see it as separate from the self**. This may be easy to do for some clients, while for others, this step may require a

metaphorical, imagined, or actual unraveling of SELF from the clutches of the addiction pattern program/matrix.

GAMPS STEP FOUR—
KNOWING THE SPACE
BETWEEN THE ADDICTION AND THE SELF:

And then the next step calls us. Once we (our clients, ourselves) are differentiated, separated from the problem addiction pattern program (separated metaphorically or actually or both, you decide), we can not only (imagine we are or actually) **speak to this problem pattern program**, we can also (imagine we are or actually) **hear this problem pattern program respond to us.** *Even imagination versus actuality presents a conceptual Paradox for ourselves.* Let this level and energy of *Paradox* reverberate throughout the SELF, feel what this means. Come to know the energy of *Paradox*. Begin to feel the energy held in *Paradox,* in problem addiction patterning traps.

GAMPS STEP FIVE—
THE MATRIX GESTALTING ITSELF:

Now the highly aware psychotherapist, clinician, guide, can see, sense, feel, the moment when the client comes face to face with the problem addiction matrix that has moved into the programming, the brain, the neural wiring of this client. This is also a **coming face to face with *Paradox*** (as per *Chapters 13* and *17*). Here is where the psychotherapist's (or other guide's) modeling and guidance can allow this client to meet the invader, the addiction program, come face to face with the problem addiction, and **"see" (sense, feel, know, generate) the conceptual, virtual** *space between the addiction and the SELF*. Here is where conceiving of, working on developing, a boundary between the SELF and the problem addiction program/matrix intertwining with the SELF is a valuable visualization type of exercise. Here is where we all can feel the *power of the gestalt*ING, of the *realization and release.*

This newly defined boundary between the SELF and the addiction program/matrix draws a line right through the *Paradox* of the muddled Identity that the problem addiction matrix has generated within us.

GAMPS STEP SIX—
CONSCIOUS AWARENESS
AND UNDERSTANDING
OF THE MATRIX AND ITS WORKINGS:
Now these understandings make more and more sense to us:

1) The dialog toward the long and lasting learning of the sustained AHA, the sustained *Elevation* in awareness, begins. Help clients understand that for AHA *Insights* to be sustained, to truly result in lasting *Elevations* in awareness, in learning, understanding, and even in behavior, momentary *Insights* must themselves be repeated, practiced, sustained. This slow and repeated consciously experienced AHA *Insight* leads to sustained *Elevation*.
2) We can recognize more and more about our problem patterns. We can tag these patterns with characteristics as they move through our minds/brains, the way scientists may tag animals in the wild to track them.
3) We can speak to our problem patterns and hear these patterns and their matrices speak to us.
4) In so doing, we can *further differentiate ourselves* from problem addiction pattern programs/matrices.
5) Already, just by initiating this understanding, this problem pattern program/matrix is *GestaltING itself*. Just by being present for this, by having us feel its presence, it is acknowledging its presence.
6) Anything this problem addiction pattern does or does not do in this process is the problem pattern *GestaltING itself*:

- If this problem pattern does <u>not</u> respond when we address it, it reveals its programming to remain hidden, under our conscious radar. Yet, we have already identified it and put it at least conceptually outside of ourselves to confront it.
- If this problem pattern <u>does</u> respond (whether this response is imaginary or actual), anything it responds with is also a *gestalt of itself*.

> **Basically, we have double binded our own problem addiction program/matrix, gestalted the Trojan Horse out from under the radar, out from under the cloak of invisibility on which it rode into us!!!**

7) Like figures in an Escher print, the voice of the problem pattern program/matrix now comes out of the ground (and background), out of the woodwork, *reveals itself,* already *GestaltING itself* in its self revealing. This *GestaltING* is its *Reality/Form Completion* of itself, as seeing more of the whole picture reveals the invader, the problem addiction program/matrix. (Once the infection is detected, the infected picture it forms can be refused, revised, its representation of reality detected and confronted.)

8) Where this problem pattern has delved very deeply into our own Identity, now this *GestaltING Process* is revealing the presence, the Identity, of the problem addiction pattern itself—and confirming that:

the SELF is
<u>NOT</u> THIS
PROBLEM ADDICTION
PATTERN/PROGRAM/MATRIX.

THE ART OF ORCHESTRATING THE TRANSFORMATIONAL JUXTAPOSITION

The highly aware psychotherapist/clinician/guide can generate and then see, sense, feel, the moment when the client comes face to face with the problem addiction program matrix/presence that has moved into the programming, the neural wiring of the client.

Here is where adept guidance can allow this client to meet the addiction program/matrix, and then to come face to face with the conceptual, virtual space—and boundary—between the addiction program matrix and the SELF. Again, conceiving of a space and then a boundary between the SELF and the problem addiction program/matrix afflicting the SELF is key in this process.

Realization and then release is learned and acquired. We learn we can SEE THE HIDDEN FACE OF ADDICTION, see the problem pattern/matrix that it is. We understand we can DETECT AND CONFRONT THIS INVASIVE PRESENCE.

TRUE PROBLEM/CHALLENGE: TAKE YOURSELF BACK FROM THIS INVASIVE PROBLEM ADDICTION PATTERN PROGRAM/MATRIX

THE PROBLEM PATTERN'S GOAL IS TO MERGE WITH THE HOST, WITH THE PERSON, TO FULLY INSTATE ITSELF AS THE DOMINANT PATTERN WITHIN ITS HOST.
The trigger-urge-craving addicted response cycle (pattern) below is NOT the host's pattern, it is the invasive problem addiction's pattern/program.

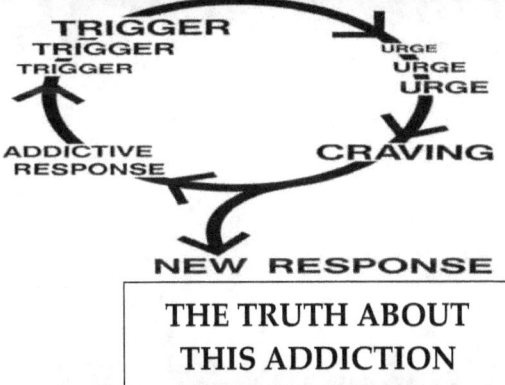

THE TRUTH ABOUT THIS ADDICTION

**THE SELF MUST FULLY KNOW AND LIVE THE TRUTH WHICH IS:
I, THE HOST, AM NOT THIS INVASIVE PROBLEM ADDICTION PATTERN/PROGRAM.
I MUST DO EVERYTHING I CAN, NOW THAT I KNOW THIS, TO TAKE MYSELF BACK FROM THIS INVADER.**

Here is the **JUXTAPOSITION PRESSURE** we have now placed on this invader, this problem addiction pattern programming: NOW ADDICTION, I SEE YOU, you are called out now, *you are caught in your own Paradoxical double bind*, the one you have been programming me to stay trapped in, to not see the existence of. **I AM NOT YOU.**
I WILL HOLD YOU BACK, STOP YOU NOW.

Part Four

Let's No Longer Be Blocked From Seeing This

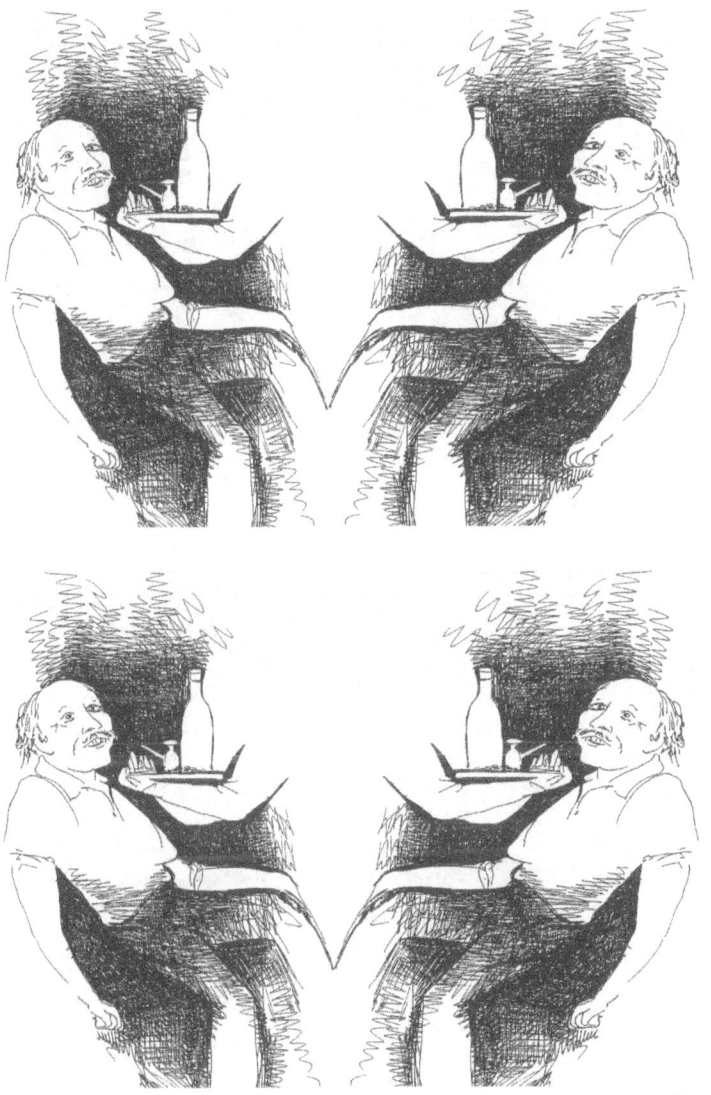

FACINGS

20
No Longer Be Programmed To Be Oblivious

Virtually oblivious to the presence of the *problem addiction program matrix*, and to the trapping *Paradoxical **double bind patterning*** it instills to ***hold itself in place within us***, many of us—lay persons and professionals, clinicians, practitioners, researchers, policy makers—proceed in our/their lives and work.

Indeed, much of the excellent and well meaning addiction therapy and addiction treatment seeks to promote healthy changes in behavior, and does so quite intently while not addressing in depth (if at all) this concept, this invasive problem addiction ***program/matrix*** defined in this book, SEEING THE HIDDEN FACE OF ADDICTION. [44] (Of course and most certainly, the linking of the emotional with the cognitive processes is being done very well in a range of treatment and therapy contexts.[45] This book does not criticize these approaches, rather seeks to underscore, augment, and bring to a new level of understanding and awareness the work being done.)

I do want to note here, even to highlight and emphasize here, that it is time we do address: the ***GestaltING of the deeply embedded***

---

[44] See more in the books where I further delve into my views and theories such as NAVIGATING LIFE'S STUFF, also OVERRIDING THE EXTINCTION SCENARIO, Part One, and TRANSCENDING ADDICTION AND OTHER AFFLICTIONS, and GESTALTING ADDICTION—SPEAKING TRUTH TO ADDICTION.

[45] Examples include CBT, Cognitive Behavioral Therapy, and DBT, Dialectical Behavioral Therapy, and their original version, RET, Rational Emotive Therapy.

addiction program/matrix; and, the <u>catalytic nature</u> of actually GestaltING the presence of (idea of, reality of) the addiction program/matrix itself.

It is time to ever more *adeptly utilize GestaltING Processes I share herein and realize their maximum positive potential.* It is time that authentic and highly informed professional training in this realm, addressing the *Patterning Awareness*, the *Reality/Form Completion*, the *Going Conscious*, and the *GestaltING Processes* I have presented herein, be made available.

I have shared some of my journey in this book, for me a journey of the intellect, the heart, and the soul. My goal is to further open minds and hearts and souls to new views, new possibilities, new understandings of what we are doing—and of who we are, of who we really are. This is just an introduction to my thinking. I will share more upon contact….

With sincere gratitude to my dear clients whose processes, recoveries, and openings to new levels of themselves, their own hearts, minds, and souls, inspires me and brings tears to my eyes almost every day. I want to honor your journeys through the Human heart, mind, and soul.

Dr. Angela®
Dr. Angela Brownemiller

21
Epilog:
The Truth About Us

If we listen, we can hear. We Humans are calling ourselves to see what is happening to us, within us, around us. We are speaking to ourselves from deep inside ourselves, telling ourselves to pay attention to the messages we are sending ourselves.

If we listen we can hear ourselves calling us to be as clear and honest with ourselves about ourselves, about who and what we are, as we can be — *and* to be as clear and honest with ourselves about those around us, about who and what these persons (and *theses persons' patterns*) are, as we can be.

This is not an easy calling. The answers are not readily found and applied. In fact, just when we think we see the whole picture, or something close to the whole picture, we do not. There is always more to know, there are always more dots to connect, there is always another segment of the whole, of the form of the SELF — to find, to discover, to call forth, to ***reality/form complete***.

The circle of our search is always infinite. The closer we get to answers, to completing the search, the closer we are to knowing we will always have more to discover. (We know, we do now, yet there are so many times we do not know we know.)

Just as we think we are finally completing the *puzzle of self*, we see (or sense on some level even when we deny this) that there are more pieces still to be discovered, that there is not yet a completion of the whole picture. No matter how close we are to completing the picture, solving the *riddle of ourselves*, there is always more to see and know, there are always more dots to connect.

This infinite *search for* (and its antithetical partner, **denial of**) the truth about ourselves reveals itself in so many ways. We find we are creatures living with incomplete knowledge about ourselves, even while telling ourselves (or being told, or our brains telling us) that: we know so much about, or know enough to see, what's going on — we see the picture, maybe even the whole picture. *Yet, we are mistaken; we do not see more than a fraction of reality.* In essence, we are trapped in a never complete picture of ourselves, our realities, our behaviors. And we become hooked on this incomplete picture, dependent upon it for sustenance. (At least we believe in our existence enough to at least believe we exist.)

In this sense, Human beings tend to even consciously choose to tell themselves that: they know what is going on, they see the whole (or enough of the whole) picture, therefore their conclusions about their inner and outer realities are accurate. Nevertheless, anything our brains tell us we know is merely a construction of a picture based on pieces of the whole reality. And, based on this book's discussion of **INFECTED REALITY/FORM COMPLETION**, what we construct to give ourselves a sense of our reality, even of ourselves, may be *contaminated by an agenda not of our own making: the agenda of the problem addiction program/matrix.*

Yes, we Humans tend to believe what our brains are wired to tell us to believe, to take what data we have and paste it together to form a picture of reality.

We do this for the sake of living within that picture. All Human beings are carrying around brains that are wired to support their belief in whatever incomplete picture they ascribe to, to tell themselves they live within a complete picture when they know, they truly know, there is no completing. The *circle of self* never closes, is always evolving, discovering. *It is this infinite* **DISCOVERY** *that is our journey.*

We Humans are wired to become addicted to ways of being, seeing, feeling, living, behaving. In this sense, we are all addicted to our realities or to what we have come to believe are our realities. Much of this addiction has great survival value. And much of this addiction does not have survival value, may actually be quite counter survival. Differentiating between healthy addictions and their patterns and unhealthy (problem) addictions and their patterns is essential and must be continuous.

So here we are, beings who know what we think we know, based on our completion of an incomplete picture, based on our brain's reading of incomplete data to tell us we know what we think we know. ... And our brains, they are working so hard to captain this ship, the ship of US, to hold us whole in the face of so many invasions of our boundaries, of our identities, of our SELVES.

Let's join together in this understanding of all that our species is facing, the challenges to our survival both:
- in external biospheric and political environments, and
- in our internal spiritual and biological, even synaptic, environments where the struggle for our survival is equally momentous.

> Praying for the future of humanity,
> and for those
> who have not survived this Earthly passage,
> and for everyone else who is or may be here.
> Every moment matters,
>
> Dr. Angela®

printed with permission, anonymous art therapy workshop participant

BOOKLIST AND RECOMMENDED READING
Some of the books by Dr. Angela Brownemiller include:

****

Interdimensional Psychology:
Psyche, Mind, and SELF Seen Through the Looking Glass

****

The Going Conscious Process:
Steps and Practices for Heightening Conscious
Awareness, Shifts, Transmigrations of Focus, LEAPs of Self

****

Overriding the Extinction Scenario, Part II:
Raising the Bar on the Evolution of the Human Species

****

Overriding the Extinction Scenario, Part I:
Detecting the Bar on the Evolution of the Human Species

****

How to Die and Survive:
Interdimensional Psychology, Consciousness, and Survival:
Concepts for Living and Dying

****

Unveiling the Hidden Instinct:
Understanding Our
Interdimensional Survival Awareness

****

Keys to Self: Your Next Steps to YOU

****

Keys to Personal Discovery:
Primer for Life's Minor and Major Challenges and Passages

****

Transcending Addiction and Other Afflictions

****

For Knowing No Hurt No Harm:
Hidden, Subtle, and Obvious Aspects of
Intimate and Other Partner
Abuse, Violence, and Terror

****

GestaltING Addiction:
Speaking Truth to Addiction –
Its Power, Definition, Theory, Therapy, and Treatment

****

Seeing the Hidden Face of Addiction:
Detecting and Confronting this Invasive Presence

See also...

International Collection on Addictions (four volumes)
Editor, Angela Brownemiller (Browne-miller)
Volume One: Faces of Addiction Then And Now
Volume Two: Psychobiological Profiles
Volume Three: Characteristics and Treatment Perspectives
Volume Four: Behavioral Addictions from Concept to Compulsion

Violence and Abuse in Society (four volumes)
Editor, Angela Brownemiller (Browne-miller)
Volume One: Fundamentals, Effects, and Extremes
Volume Two: Setting, Age, Gender, and Other Key Elements
Volume Three: Psychological, Ritual, Sexual, and Trafficking Issues
Volume Four: Faces of Intimate Partner Violence

Note:
The books listed on this and the previous page have been listed on Amazon.com. If not finding these books on Amazon.com, contact local or online bookstores, and or Amazon.com, and or DrAngela@DrAngela.com for the author's staff and or the author, Dr. Angela Brownemiller. Note again, this author's last name also appears as Browne-Miller.

ABOUT THE AUTHOR
Dr. Angela Brownemiller
Dr. Angela®

Dr. Angela Brownemiller, also known as Dr. Angela® (and Angela Browne-Miller), is an author, journalist, social thinker, clinician, psychotherapist, speaker, host of the Dr. Angela Hour®, and founder of the Keys to Self® Program. The views of Dr. Angela® Brownemiller are centered on the great potential of the Human mind, heart, spirit, and soul, and on the rights of all of us, who and whatever we are (or think we are). Dr. Angela Brownemiller views the Human consciousness as a wealth of opportunity for exploration, Insight, knowledge—and survival. For more information on her work, see DrAngela.com.

The works of Dr. Angela Brownemiller
(some of which are listed on the previous pages)
are brought to you by:
METATERRA® PUBLICATIONS
and other publishers.

To take part in our
online and on-ground events, workshops, and trainings
contact us at:
DrAngela@DrAngela.com
For personal consultations
in person, or by telephone, or online,
contact us at
DrAngela@DrAngela.com

www.DrAngela.com